Release the Power of

PRAYER

D0167835

Release the Power of

PRAYER

George Müller

Whitaker House

Unless otherwise indicated, all Scripture quotations are taken from the *New King James Version* (NKJV), © 1979, 1980, 1982 by Thomas Nelson, Inc. Used by permission. All rights reserved.

Scripture quotations marked (KJV) are taken from the *King James Version* of the Bible.

Whitaker House gratefully acknowledges the assistance of Julian P. Marsh, Chief Executive of The George Müller Foundation, 7 Cotham Park, Bristol BS6, 6DA, England, in providing information for the final chapter.

RELEASE THE POWER OF PRAYER
(originally titled *How God Answers Prayer*)

ISBN: 0-88368-352-0
Printed in the United States of America
Copyright © 1999 by Whitaker House

Whitaker House
30 Hunt Valley Circle
New Kensington, PA 15068

Müller, George, 1805–1898.
   Release the power of prayer / by George Müller.
      p.   cm.
   ISBN 0-88368-352-0 (trade paper)
      1. Prayer—Christianity. 2. Müller, George, 1805–1898. I. Title.
BV220 .M85 1999
289.9—dc21   99-055750

1 2 3 4 5 6 7 8 9 10 11 12 13 / 09 08 07 06 05 04 03 02 01 00

Contents

Events in George Müller's Life 6

Introduction 9

1. Early Days of the Orphan Work 21

2. The New Orphanages at Ashley Down 57

3. Precious Answers to Prayer 71

4. Conditions of Prevailing Prayer 101

5. Müller's Method of Reading the Scriptures 107

6. How to Determine the Will of God 115

7. Proving the Acceptable Will of God 119

8. God's Way 125

9. Advice on Rising Early 129

10. Müller's Ninetieth Birthday 137

11. A God-Glorifying Testimony 141

12. The Ministry Continues 145

Events in George Müller's Life

September 27, 1805   Born in Kroppenstaedt, Prussia

1810   Family moves to Heimershleben

1825   Enters Halle University to study theology

November 1825   Becomes a Christian

March 19, 1829   Arrives in London to prepare for missionary work with the London Society for Promoting Christianity among the Jews

1829   Becomes associated with founders of the Brethren movement

1830   Becomes pastor of Ebenezer Chapel in Teignmouth, England

October 7, 1830   Marries Mary Groves

October 1830   Tells congregation that he will no longer accept a regular salary

May 1832   Begins his ministry in Bristol, along with Henry Craik

September 17, 1832   Lydia, his first child, is born

March 5, 1834   Founds the Scriptural Knowledge Institution for Home and Abroad

March 19, 1834   Elijah, his son, is born

June 25, 1835   Elijah dies from pneumonia

April 11, 1836   First orphanage at 6 Wilson Street opens

November 28, 1836   Second house on Wilson Street opens

September 1837   Third house on Wilson Street opens

1841   His father dies

Events in George Müller's Life

July 1844	Fourth house on Wilson Street opens
June 1849	First orphanage at Ashley Down opens
November 1857	Second building at Ashley Down opens
March 1862	Third building at Ashley Down opens
January 22, 1866	Henry Craik dies
November 1868	Fourth building at Ashley Down opens
January 1870	Fifth building at Ashley Down opens
February 6, 1870	Mary, his first wife, dies
1870	Lydia Müller marries James Wright
1870s	Sends £10,000 annually to nearly two hundred missionaries
November 30, 1871	Müller marries Susannah Grace Sangar
1875	Begins preaching tours, which take him to 42 countries, traveling 200,000 miles to preach to 3 million people
1878	Meets President Hayes and tours the White House
January 10, 1890	Daughter Lydia dies
May 1892	Final preaching tour
January 13, 1894	Susannah, his second wife, dies
June 1897	Preaches at Bethesda Chapel
March 6, 1898	Preaches his last sermon at Alma Road Chapel in Clifton
March 10, 1898	Dies peacefully at the age of 92

Introduction*

George Müller was born in Kroppenstaedt, Prussia, on September 27, 1805. His father, a tax collector, educated his children in worldly principles, and George and his brother slipped easily into many sins. Before he was ten years old, he had repeatedly stolen government money, which had been entrusted to his father. His father was forced to make up the losses.

When George was eleven years old, his father sent him to Halberstadt to prepare to study at the university. His father wanted him to become a clergyman— not so that he would serve God, but rather that he would earn a comfortable living. George's favorite pastimes were studying, reading novels, and indulging in sinful practices.

His mother died suddenly when he was only fourteen years old. On the night of her death, he played cards until two in the morning, then went to a tavern the next day. His love of liquor was stronger than his ties to his mother.

Three days before his confirmation and communion, he was guilty—as he later admitted—of "gross immorality." On the day prior to his confirmation, he

---

* Extracted from *The Autobiography of George Müller,* published by Whitaker House (1984).

lied to the clergyman rather than confess his sins. He broke his resolutions to change almost as fast as he could make them.

When George was sixteen, he was imprisoned for four weeks for running up bills at an expensive hotel and trying to escape without paying them. His father came to his rescue, but beat him severely before taking him home.

George convinced his father to give him another chance. He was allowed to enter school at Nordhausen and lived in the home of the principal of the school. He fooled the principal into thinking he was a model student, but inwardly he was as wicked as ever. His efforts at self-reform were short-lived and ineffective.

At age 20, he entered Halle University to study theology. Although he obtained permission to preach in the Lutheran church, he was as unhappy and as far from God as ever before. His life in the seminary epitomized these words of the apostle Paul: *"For the good that I will to do, I do not do; but the evil I will not to do, that I practice"* (Rom. 7:19).

A Remarkable Conversion

On a Saturday afternoon, in November 1825, George took a walk with his friend Beta. His friend told him about a prayer meeting he had been attending at a private home, where they read the Bible, sang, prayed, and read a printed sermon.* When George heard Beta's words, he felt as if he had found the treasure he had been seeking for his whole life. Together they went to the meeting that evening.

---

* At this time in Prussia, it was illegal for a sermon to be preached unless an ordained elder was present.

Introduction

As he was welcomed into the home, George observed a joy among the believers that he did not understand. For the first time in his life, he saw someone kneel in prayer. That made a deep impression on him, and while brother Kayser prayed, George thought, "I could not pray as well, although I have more education than this man."

After leaving the meeting, he felt happy, although he did not understand why. No former pleasure in life matched the joy he experienced during the prayer meeting. God began a work of grace in his heart, and that evening became a turning point in his life.

He continued to visit at this Christian brother's house and could hardly wait for Saturday to come around so that once again he could study God's Word and pray with believers. Although he did not give up every sin at once, he quit spending time with wicked companions and no longer went to the tavern. Even his habit of lying was broken. He began to attend church for the right motives, and he openly confessed Christ, despite the ridicule from his fellow students.

Müller's Missionary Zeal

As George read missionary letters, he began to feel led to be a missionary himself. Desiring to serve the Lord fully and without reservation, George wanted to share his newfound joy with others. He became concerned about the spiritual state of his father and brother. Hoping that they would embrace faith in Christ, he wrote to them. Sadly, they replied with an angry letter.

About that time, Dr. Friedrich Tholuck, a professor of divinity, came to teach at Halle University. Because of Tholuck's coming to the school, several

Christian students transferred from other schools in order to study with him. These believers helped to strengthen George's faith, and his desire to serve as a missionary intensified.

Once again he wrote to his father for the needed permission to be admitted to one of the German missionary institutions. His father said that he would no longer consider George his son if he pursued this course. He had hoped that George would become a minister and that he could live with him in the parsonage, spending his last days in comfort. Since George could not guarantee that he would fulfill his father's plans for him, he felt that he should no longer accept his father's financial support—even though he needed the money to finish two more years of seminary.

God enabled George to meet his expenses by teaching German to several American professors who had come to Halle to do literary research. George experienced the rich blessings of God as a result of what he considered to be a small sacrifice for Christ's sake. A short while later, he met Hermann Ball, a wealthy man who chose to work among the Jews in Poland rather than live in comfort with his family. Ball's commitment made a deep impression on George, and a desire to be a missionary to the Jews was born in his heart.

Tholuck informed George that the Continental Society in England intended to send a minister to Bucharest to help an aging missionary with the work of the Lord. After careful consideration and prayer, George offered to go. Unexpectedly, his father gave his consent.

As he was preparing to go to Bucharest, George learned that Hermann Ball, the missionary to the Polish Jews, was going to have to give up his work because of poor health. George felt a burning desire to take Ball's place, but he had promised to go to Bucharest.

Introduction

Calling on Dr. Tholuck one day, George was asked by his professor if he had ever had a desire to work among the Jews. He was astonished by the question and told Tholuck that the desire to do so had been on his mind for several weeks. Both agreed, though, that he had made a commitment to go to Bucharest, which needed to be honored.

By the next morning, all of George's desire to go to Bucharest was gone. He prayed for God to restore it, which He did. Meanwhile, George's earnest study of Hebrew was becoming a passion.

About ten days later, Tholuck learned that because of the war between the Turks and the Russians, the missionary society had decided not to send a minister to Bucharest. Once again he asked George what he thought about becoming a missionary to the Jews.

After prayer and godly counsel, George decided to offer himself for service to the London Society for Promoting Christianity among the Jews. Through Dr. Tholuck's help, George was accepted as a missionary student by the London Society.

Through God's miraculous intervention, George was exempted from Prussian military duty for life because of a tendency to tuberculosis, and he received his passport, which enabled him to travel to England. God's plans for using George Müller in ways that he had never dreamed were just beginning.

Weakness Becomes Strength

When George arrived in England, he was physically weak, and he became so ill that he thought he would not recover. In a way that only God's people

13

would understand, he experienced a peace within his spirit, even though he was becoming weaker in his body. As he thought about the sins that he had committed and realized the forgiving grace he had received from the Lord, he was at peace. He was ready to die and be with the Lord forever if that was God's plan for him.

When the doctor came, George prayed, "Lord, You know that he does not know what is best for me. Therefore, please direct him." As George took the medicine prescribed for him, his prayer was, "Lord, You know that this medicine is no more than a little water. Now please, Lord, let it produce the effect that is for my good and for Your glory. Let me either soon be taken to heaven, or let me be restored. Lord, do with me as You think best!"

God's will was for George to be returned to health, but He still had lessons to teach him during his illness. Friends invited him to the country to recuperate, and this opportunity gave him a great deal of time to study the Bible.

The Master Teacher

God's lessons were rich and deep. He showed George that His Word was to be the "standard of judgment," and that the Holy Spirit would be his teacher. He was led to lay aside his commentaries and almost every other book so that he could simply study the Bible. He said that in the first evening that he looked to the Word of God alone, he learned more in a few hours than he had learned during the last several months.

When he returned to London, he purposed to give what strength he had to the work of the Lord. He wanted to leave immediately as a missionary, but he received no reply from his request to the mission society that he be sent out. Rather than waiting for official recognition, he felt that he should begin to serve God right where he was—with or without the title of missionary. He began to distribute tracts to the Jews in London, and soon he was reading the Scriptures on a regular basis with about fifty Jewish boys.

As 1829 came to a close, George felt that he should not be supported financially by the London Society. He felt that he should look only to the Lord for direction and provision. With no ill regard on either side, George dissolved his relationship with the society and now felt free to preach the Gospel wherever the Lord opened the doors.

Absolute Reliance on God

God led the way for George to become the pastor of the eighteen-member chapel in Teignmouth. Here God taught him how to rely on His direction as to what to preach to the people. He learned early that "only a life of prayer and meditation will render a vessel ready for the Master's use." He learned that without God's blessing, direction, and presence, he could accomplish nothing, but through relying on God, he could claim the promise from Philippians 4:13: *"I can do all things through Christ who strengthens me."*

While at Teignmouth, George met and married Mary Groves. God also led him to refuse to take a specific salary, although he did appreciate the support of his parishioners. He realized the influence people's status could have over his ministry, and he never wanted to be tempted to compromise preaching the full Gospel because of wanting to avoid offending those who were paying his salary. In addition, he felt that the practice of renting the pews in the church was not scriptural. Those who had more money could afford the choice seats, while the poorer members could not. He and Mary agreed that a box would be placed in the chapel. A sign on it would explain that those who wished to support the pastor could put an offering in the box. That way he would never know who was giving money for their support or how much money any individual was giving. God blessed this step of faith, and their needs were always provided. George Müller was just beginning to walk a path that would lead him to greater dependence on God and greater joy in seeing God answer all of his prayers. The lessons of faith learned at Teignmouth would lead him to greater steps of faith when they moved to Bristol.

After two years and three months at Teignmouth, George began to feel that his work there would soon be completed. With sadness at leaving the people he had come to love, but being fully persuaded that it was God's will, George and Mary arrived in Bristol on May 25, 1832.

The Ministry Expands

Along with Henry Craik, George Müller became the pastor at Gideon Chapel. Another opportunity presented itself when he and Craik were offered the Bethesda Chapel. A man offered to pay the rent on the building for one year, so Craik and Müller agreed to preach at that church as well. God added 109 people to these fellowships during the first year of their ministry in Bristol. Sixty-five were new converts, and many were backsliders who had returned to serving the Lord. Between sixty and eighty people a day came to receive bread, until the neighbors complained about the beggars loitering in the streets. George had to tell the people that they could no longer receive bread, but his desire to help the poor only increased.

During February 1834, God began to lead George in forming an institution that would be established to spread the Gospel at home and abroad. Although other organizations were already working toward the same purposes, George felt led to found a group that would not "seek the patronage of the world." It was his purpose that God alone would be their patron, and "if He [was] not on [their] side, [they would] not succeed." No unbelievers would be involved in managing the affairs of the institution, and no money would be sought from "unconverted people of rank or wealth to support this institution because [he] believe[d] this would be dishonorable to the Lord."

By June of the following year, five day schools had been established for teaching 439 poor children; 795 Bibles and 753 New Testaments had been distributed; and financial and prayer support had been given to missionaries in Canada, the East Indies, and Europe.

Even so, George Müller was not content to think that God had accomplished all He was going to do through him. He began to dream about establishing a house for orphans, and on November 21, 1835, he felt led to begin making plans. On April 11, 1836, the first house was opened at 6 Wilson Street to care for seventeen children. Soon thirty girls lived with the Müllers. Before long, George bought a second house at 1 Wilson

Street, which was soon filled with thirty infants. A third house at 3 Wilson Street came available the next year, and it became home to about forty boys, seven years of age or older. The ministry at the orphan homes on Wilson Street expanded until the need to relocate became inevitable. Eventually, God would multiply the work until it would touch the lives of over ten thousand orphans. God transformed George Müller, a little boy who stole from his earthly father, into a man who could be trusted with the resources of his heavenly Father.

That the genuineness of your faith, being much more precious than gold that perishes, though it is tested by fire, may be found to praise, honor, and glory at the revelation of Jesus Christ.
—1 Peter 1:7

Chapter One

Early Days
of the Orphan Work

Although George Müller had felt a call to the mission field, God chose to bring the mission field to him. He laid it upon George's heart to testify to the faithfulness of God by providing for orphans. Always concerned about the poor and the orphaned, he was even more burdened to minister to unbelievers. In the first volume of his book, *A Narrative of Some of the Lord's Dealings with George Müller,* he described what prompted him to begin the orphan work:

Sometimes children of God are afraid of the prospect of growing old and becoming unable to work any longer. They are harassed by the fear of being poor and incapable of providing for themselves. If I point out to them how their heavenly Father has always helped those who put their trust in Him, they might not go so far as to say, "Times have changed," yet it is evident that they do not look upon God as the living God. My spirit was often burdened by observing such Christians' lack of faith, and I longed to set something before these children of God so that they might see that He does not forsake, even in our day, those who rely upon Him.

Another segment of God's people whom I saw experiencing internal conflict was Christian businessmen. They often brought guilt upon their consciences by conducting their businesses almost in the same way as unconverted persons do. Competition in trade, bad times, and overpopulation were given as reasons why a business run according to the Word of God could not be expected to do well. Such a businessman, perhaps, expressed the wish that his situation could be different. However, before I began my orphan work, very rarely did I see someone in business taking a stand for God, showing a holy determination to trust in the living God, or depending on Him in order to maintain a good conscience. Therefore, I desired to show to these people, by a visible proof, that God is unchangeably the same.

Other individuals were in professions in which they could not continue if they wanted to keep a clear conscience. These persons were in an unscriptural position with regard to spiritual things. Knowing that they could not continue in their positions while abiding in fellowship with God, they still refused to change their professions or to leave their current positions lest they become unemployed. My spirit longed to be instrumental in strengthening their faith, by not only giving them instances from the Word of God of His willingness and ability to help all those who rely upon Him, but also showing them by visible proofs that God is the same in our day.

I well knew that the Word of God ought to be enough, and it was, by grace, enough for me. Still, I considered that I ought to lend a helping hand to my brothers, if, by any means, by this visible proof of the unchangeable faithfulness of the Lord, I might strengthen their faith in God. I remembered what a great blessing my own soul had received through seeing the result of the Lord's dealings with His servant A. H. Francke,* who, in dependence upon the living God alone, established an immense orphanage. Since I had seen this visible proof of God's faithfulness many times with my own eyes, I felt bound to be the servant of the church of God in the same way through which I had obtained mercy: namely, in being able to take God by His Word and to rely upon it.

All these exercises of my soul, which resulted from the fact that so many believers with whom I had become acquainted were harassed and distressed in mind, or had guilty consciences from not trusting in the Lord, were used by God to awaken in my heart the desire to set before the church at large, and before the world, proof that He has not changed in the least. The best way to testify to God's faithfulness seemed to be to establish an orphanage. It needed to be something that could be seen, even by the natural eye.

Now, if I, a poor man, simply by prayer and faith, obtained the means for establishing and running an orphanage without asking for help from any individual, that would be something that, with the Lord's blessing, might be instrumental in strengthening the faith of the children of God. Additionally, it would be a testimony to the consciences of the unconverted to the reality of the things of God. This, then, was the primary reason for establishing an orphanage.

---

* While a divinity student at Halle University, Müller lived for two months in free housing provided by the Orphan House built by August H. Francke one hundred years earlier. Although Francke died in 1727, his dependence upon God and his work on behalf of orphans greatly influenced Müller.

Certainly, I desired to be used by God to benefit the poor children who had been bereaved of both parents, and to seek, in other respects, with the help of God, to do them good in this life. I also particularly longed to be used by God in training the dear orphans in the fear of God. Still, the first and primary objective of the work was, and still is, that God might be magnified by the fact that the orphans under my care are provided with all they need only by prayer and faith—without anyone being asked by me or my fellow workers for resources, so that God's faithfulness might be seen. Through His provision, others would see that He still hears and answers prayer.

That I was not mistaken has been abundantly proved since November 1835, both by the conversion of many sinners who have read the accounts that have been published in connection with this work, and also by the abundance of fruit that has followed in the hearts of the saints. From my inmost soul, I desire to be grateful to God for His provision. The honor and glory is due to Him alone, and, by His help, I am enabled to ascribe the praise to Him.

Open Your Mouth Wide

In the account written by George Müller on January 16, 1836, we see his dependence on the leading of God as he sought to know and to obey God's will in regard to establishing the orphanages in Bristol. We read:

When, of late, the thoughts of establishing an orphanage, in dependence upon the Lord, revived in my mind, during the first two weeks I only prayed that if it were of the Lord, He would bring it about. If not, I prayed that He graciously would be pleased to take all thoughts about it from my mind. My uncertainty about knowing the Lord's mind did not arise from questioning whether it would be pleasing in His sight for there to be a home and scriptural education provided for destitute, fatherless and motherless children. My question was whether it was His will for me to be the instrument of setting such a purpose on foot, since my hands were already more than filled.

My comfort, however, was that, if it was His will, He would provide not merely the means, but also suitable individuals to take care of the children. That way, my part of the work would take only such a portion of my time as, considering the importance of the matter, I might give, notwithstanding my many other engagements. The whole of those two weeks I never asked the Lord for money or for persons to engage in the work.

On December 5, however, the subject of my prayer all at once became different. I was reading Psalm 81 and was particularly struck, more than at any time before, with verse 10: *"Open your mouth wide, and I will fill it."* I thought a few moments about these words, and then was led to apply them to the case of the orphanage. It struck me that I had never asked the Lord for anything concerning it, except to know His will, regarding its being established or not. I then fell on my knees and opened my mouth wide, asking Him for much. I asked in submission to His will, without setting a time when He should answer my petition. I prayed that He would give me a house, either as a loan or that someone might be led to pay the rent for one, or that one might be given permanently for this purpose. Further, I asked Him for £1000 and for suitable individuals to take care of the children. Besides this, I have been led since to ask the Lord to put it into the hearts of His people to send articles of furniture for the house and some clothing for the children.

When I was asking the petition, I was fully aware of what I was doing: I was asking for something that I had no natural prospect of obtaining from the people whom I knew, but which was not too much for the Lord to grant.

Within a few days, Müller began to see God's answers to prayer. He recorded the following entries in his journal:

December 10, 1835. This morning I received a letter in which a brother and sister wrote these words: "We offer ourselves for the service of the intended orphanage, if you think we are qualified. Also, we will donate all the furniture that the Lord has given to us, for use in the orphanage. We want to do this without receiving any salary whatever, believing that if it is the will of the Lord to employ us, He will supply all our needs."

December 13. A brother was influenced this day to give 4s. per week, or £10 8s. yearly, as long as the Lord supplies the means; 8s. was given by him as two weeks' subscriptions. Today a brother and sister offered themselves, with all their furniture, and all the provisions that they have in their house, if they can be usefully employed in the concerns of the orphanage.

God Provides Encouragement

In spite of these answers to prayer, Müller was not immune to discouragement. He wrote in his journal,

December 17. I was rather cast down last evening and this morning, questioning whether I ought to be engaged in this way, and was led to ask the Lord to give me some further encouragement. Soon after a brother sent me two pieces of material, one seven yards in length and the other 23¾ yards of calico. He also donated four pieces of lining, which are about four yards altogether, a sheet, and a yard measure. This evening another brother brought a clotheshorse, three frocks, four pinafores, six handkerchiefs, three quilts, one blanket, two pewter saltcellars, six tin cups, and six metal teaspoons. He also brought 3s. 6d. given to him by three different individuals. At the same time, he told me that it had been put into the heart of an individual to send £100 tomorrow.

God's Faithfulness Demonstrated

Although Müller had received nearly all of the entire sum of £1000 for which he had prayed, his persistence in prayer is seen in the following journal entry:

June 15, 1837. Today I gave myself once more earnestly to prayer respecting the remainder of the £1000. This evening £5 was given, so that now the whole sum is made up. To the glory of the Lord, whose I am, and whom I serve, I state again, that every shilling of this money, and all the articles of clothing and furniture, have been given to me without one single individual having been asked by me for anything.

Another Lesson in Reliance on God

Although Müller was careful to seek God's direction even in the smallest detail, there was one thing for which he forgot to pray. He later wrote,

As far as I remember, I brought even the most minute circumstances concerning the orphanage before the Lord in my petitions, being conscious of my own weakness and ignorance. There was, however, one point I had never prayed about, namely, that the Lord would send children. I naturally took it for granted that there would be plenty of applications. However, the nearer the day came that had been appointed for receiving applications, the more I had a secret consciousness that the Lord might disappoint my natural expectations and show me that I could not prosper in one single thing without Him.

The appointed time came, and not even one application was made. Before this point, I had been repeatedly tempted to question whether I might not, after all, have engaged in the work against the Lord's will. This circumstance now led me to lie low before my God in prayer the entire evening of February 3. I examined my heart once more as to all the motives concerning the founding of the orphanage. I was able to say, as I had before, that His glory was my chief aim, that is, that it might be seen that it is not a vain thing to trust in the living God. My second aim was the spiritual welfare of the orphaned children; my third, their bodily welfare.

Continuing in prayer, I was at last brought to the state where I could say from my heart that I would rejoice in God's being glorified in this matter even if the whole thing resulted in nothing. But since it still seemed to me more tending to the glory of God to establish and prosper the orphanage, I could then heartily ask Him to send applications. I now enjoyed a peaceful state of heart concerning the subject and was also more assured than ever that God would establish it. The very next day, February 4, the first application was made, and since then forty-two more have been received.

Enough for Today

Later, when there were nearly one hundred people to care for, and the funds were very low, Müller wrote,

July 22, 1838. This evening I was walking in our little garden, meditating on Hebrews 13:8, *"Jesus Christ is the same yesterday, today, and forever."* While meditating on His unchangeable love, power, and wisdom, and, as I went on, turning all into prayer concerning myself, I applied His unchangeable love, power, and wisdom to both my present spiritual and temporal circumstances. All at once, the present need of the orphanage was brought to my mind. Immediately, I was led to say to myself,

> Jesus, in His love and power, has hitherto supplied me with what I have needed for the orphans, and in the same unchangeable love and power, He will provide me with what I may need for the future.

A flow of joy came into my soul while realizing the unchangeableness of our loving Lord. About one minute after I had this thought, a letter was brought to me. Enclosed in it was a £20 note. The letter stated,

> Will you apply the amount of the enclosed bill to the furtherance of the objectives of the Scriptural Knowledge Society, to your orphanage, or to the work and cause of our Master in

any way that He Himself, on your application to Him, may point out to you? It is not a great sum, but it is a sufficient provision for the needs of today, and it is for today's needs that, ordinarily, the Lord provides. Tomorrow, as it brings its demands, will find its supply.

Of this £20, I took £10 for the orphan fund, and £10 for the other causes, and was thus enabled to meet the expenses of about £34, which, in connection with the orphanage, came upon me within four days afterward, and which I knew beforehand would come.

Learning to Wait

Finding the needs of the orphanages great and the supply of resources low, Müller continued to trust God to supply their needs. In his journal, we read about the difficult situation he faced:

November 21, 1838. Never were we so reduced in funds as today. There was not a single halfpenny in hand among the matrons of the three houses. Nevertheless, we had a good dinner, and by sharing our bread, we made it through this day well. But we had no prospect of taking in bread for any of the houses. When I left the brothers and sisters at one o'clock, after prayer, I told them that we must wait for help, and see how the Lord would deliver us this time. I was sure of help, but we were indeed facing a serious situation.

When I came to Kingsdown, I felt that I needed more exercise since I was very cold; therefore, I did not go home by the closest route, but went by way of Clarence Place. About twenty yards from my house, I met a brother who walked the rest of the way with me. After a little conversation, he gave me £10 to provide poor believers with coal, blankets, and warm clothing. He also gave £5 for the orphans and £5 for the other needs of the Scriptural Knowledge Institution. The brother had come to see me twice while I was away at the orphanages. Had I been one half minute later, I would have missed him. But the Lord knew our need, and therefore allowed me to meet him. I sent off the £5 immediately to the matrons.

Beyond Disappointment

Müller continued to testify to the faithfulness of God. In his journal, we see his confidence in God's ability to provide:

Monday, September 21, 1840. With what was in hand for the orphans, added to what came in yesterday, the needs of today are more than supplied, and there is enough for tomorrow also. Today a brother from the neighborhood of London gave me £10 to be used as it might be most needed. Since we have been praying many days for the school, Bible, and missionary funds, I took it all for them. This brother knew nothing about our work when he came to Bristol three days ago. Thus the Lord, to show His continued care over us, raises up new helpers. Those who trust in the Lord will never be confounded (Ps. 22:5 KJV)!

Some who helped for a while may fall asleep in Jesus (1 Cor. 15:20); others may grow cold in the service of the Lord (Matt. 24:12); others may be as desirous as ever to help, but no longer have the means (see Mark 12:42–44); others may have both a willing heart and the means to help, but they may see it as the Lord's will to distribute their resources in another way. Thus, for one reason or another, if we were to lean upon man, we would surely be confounded; but, in leaning upon the living God alone, we are beyond disappointment and beyond being forsaken because of death or lack of resources or lack of love or because of the claims of other work. How precious to have learned in any measure to stand alone in the world with God and yet to be happy, and to know that surely no good thing will be withheld from us while we walk uprightly (Ps. 84:11)!

A Miraculous Conversion

Looking back on God's amazing answers to prayer during the year 1841, George Müller wrote,

During this year, I was informed about the conversion of one of the very greatest sinners that I had ever heard of in all my service for the Lord. Repeatedly, I fell on my knees, along with his wife, and asked the Lord for his conversion. She would come to me in the deepest distress of soul because of the most barbarous and cruel treatment that she received from him. He held bitter enmity against her because of her commitment to the Lord, and because he could not provoke her to be filled with rage against him. At the time when his treatment of her was at its worst, I pleaded the promise in Matthew 18:19 especially on his behalf: *"Again I say to you that if two of you agree on earth concerning anything that they ask, it will be done for them by My Father in heaven."* And now this awful persecutor is converted!

Early Days of the Orphan Work

Prayer for Spiritual Blessings

Müller recorded another answer to prayer during that year in the following account:

On May 25, I began to ask the Lord for greater spiritual prosperity among the saints with whom I labor in Bristol than there ever had been. To the praise of the Lord, I now record that truly He has answered this request, for, considering all things, at no period has there been a greater manifestation of grace and truth and spiritual power among us than there is now while I am writing this for the press (1845). It is not that we have attained to what we might (see Philippians 3:13–14); we are far, very far from it. But the Lord has been very, very good to us, and we have the most abundant reasons for thanksgiving.

Withholding the Report

In the following entry, we see how the faithful perseverance of Müller and his coworkers was tested:

December 9, 1841. Today 10s. 10d. came in for the orphans through the sale of stockings. We have now come to the close of the sixth year of this part of the work, having only in hand the money that has been saved for the rent. Throughout this whole year, we have been supplied with all that was needed.

For the last three years, we had closed the accounts on this day. We had held public meetings a few days after, at which, for the benefit of the hearers, we stated how the Lord had dealt with us during the year.

The substance of what had been stated at these meetings was afterward printed for the benefit of the church at large.

This time, however, it appeared to be better to delay the report for a while. Through grace, we had learned to lean upon the Lord only, being assured that, if we were never to speak or write one single word more about this work, we would still be supplied with means, as long as He enabled us to depend on Himself alone. We had not held those public meetings for the purpose of exposing our needs. Nor had we published the account of the Lord's dealings with us for the sake of working up the feelings of the readers, thus inducing them to give money. We had only had the meetings in order to benefit other saints by our experiences.

Yet it might have appeared to some that, in making known our circumstances, we were driven by self-serving motives. What better proof, therefore, could we give of our depending upon the living God alone and not upon public meetings or printed reports than, in the midst of our deep poverty, to continue quietly for some time longer without saying anything instead of being glad that the time had come when we could make our circumstances known?

We therefore determined, as we sought and still seek in this work to act for the profit of the saints generally, to delay for a few months both the public meetings and the report. Naturally, we would have been as glad as anyone to have revealed our poverty at that time, but spiritually we were enabled to delight even then in the prospect of the increased benefit that might be derived by the church at large from our acting as we did.

Continuing to review his circumstances during the year 1841 in both his journal and *Narrative,* Müller wrote,

December 18, Saturday morning. There is now the greatest need, and only 4d. in hand, which I found in the box at my house. Yet I fully believe that the Lord will supply us this day also with all that is required.

Pause a few moments, dear reader, and observe two things: We acted for God in delaying the public meetings and the publishing of the report, but God's way always leads into trial, as far as sight and sense are concerned. Nature will always be tried in God's ways. The Lord was saying to us by our poverty, "I will now see whether you truly lean upon Me, and whether you truly look to Me." Of all the seasons that I had ever passed through since I had been living in this way, I never knew any period in which my faith was tried as sharply as during the four months from December 12, 1841, to April 12, 1842.

But observe further: We might even then have changed our minds with respect to the public meetings and publishing the report, for no one knew our determination at this time concerning the reason for the delay. No, on the contrary, we knew with what delight many children of God were looking forward to receiving further updates. But the Lord kept us steadfast to the conclusion at which we had arrived under His guidance.

God Is Faithful

Ever concerned that his life and work would be honoring to God, George Müller wrote on January 25, 1842,

Perhaps, dear reader, you have said in your heart before you have read thus far:

How would it be if the funds for the orphans were reduced to nothing, and those who were in the work had nothing of their own to give? Suppose a mealtime arrived, and you had no food for the children?

Thus indeed it could happen, for our hearts are *"desperately wicked"* (Jer. 17:9). If we should ever be left to ourselves by either no longer depending on the living God or by allowing sin a place in our hearts (Ps. 66:18), then such a state of things, we have reason to believe, would occur. But as long as we are enabled to trust in the living God, and as long as, though falling short in every way of what we might be and ought to be, we are at least kept from living in sin, such a state of things cannot occur.

Therefore, dear reader, if you yourself walk with God, and if, on that account, His glory is dear to you, I affectionately and earnestly entreat you to beseech Him to uphold us. How awful the disgrace brought upon His holy name would be if we, who have so publicly made our boast in Him and have spoken well of Him, should be left to disgrace Him, either by unbelief in the hour of trial or by a life of sin in other respects!

The Evidence of Faith

Many times, Müller believed by faith that the answer to prayer was on its way even though he had no tangible assurance of that fact.

March 9, 1842. At a time of the greatest need, both with regard to the day schools and the orphans, so much so that we could not have gone on any longer without help, I received £10 this day from a brother who lives near Dublin. The money was divided among the day schools and the orphanages. The following circumstance is to be noticed in regard to this donation: Since our need was so great, and my soul was, through grace, truly waiting upon the Lord, I watched for supplies during the course of the morning. The mail, however, had been delivered, and no provisions had come. This did not in the least discourage me. I said to myself, "The Lord can send means without the postman. Even now, although the mail has come, through this very delivery of letters, God may have sent the answer, although the money is not yet in my hands." It was not long after I had thus spoken to myself, when, according to my hope in God, we were helped, for the brother who sent us the £10 had this time directed his letter to the boys' orphanage. From there, it had been forwarded to me.

Like a Father

Müller found the heavenly Father faithful in meeting the needs of His children.

March 17. From March 12 to March 16, £4 5s. 11 ½d. had come in for the orphans. This morning our poverty, which now has lasted more or less for several months, had become exceedingly great. I left my house a few minutes after seven to go to the orphanages to see whether there was money enough to purchase the milk, which is brought about eight o'clock. On my way, it was my special request that the Lord would be pleased to pity us, even *"as a father pities his children"* (Ps. 103:13), and that He would not lay more upon us than He would enable us to bear (1 Cor. 10:13). I especially asked Him that He would now be pleased to refresh our hearts by sending us help. Likewise, I reminded Him of the consequences that would result, both in reference to believers and unbelievers, if we should have to give up the work because of a lack of means, and that He therefore would not permit the work thus far to come to nothing. Moreover, I again confessed before the Lord that I did not deserve that He should continue to use me in this work any longer.

While I was thus in prayer, about a two minutes' walk from the orphanages, I met a brother who was going at this early hour to his business. After having exchanged a few words with him, I continued on, but presently, he ran after me and gave me £1 for the orphans. Thus the Lord speedily answered my prayer. Truly, it is worth being poor and greatly tried in faith for the sake of having day by day such precious proofs of the loving interest that our kind Father takes in everything that concerns us. And how could our Father do otherwise? He, who has given us the greatest possible proof of His love that He could have done in giving us His own Son, surely will with Him also *"freely give us all things"* (Rom. 8:32).

Another Lesson in Faith

Tempted to trust in the promises of man, George Müller discovered the peace that comes in trusting wholly upon God:

May 6, 1845. About six weeks ago intimation was kindly given by a brother that he expected a certain considerable sum of money, and that, if he obtained it, a certain portion of it would be given to the Lord, so that £100 of it might be used for the work in my hands, and the other part for brother Craik's* and my own personal expenses. However, day after day passed, and the money did not come. I did not trust in this money, yet, as during all this time, with scarcely any exception, we were more or less needy, I thought again and again about this brother's promise. Still, by the grace of God, I did not trust in the brother who had made it, but in the Lord. Week after week passed, and still the money did not come.

Now this morning it came to my mind that such promises ought to be valued, in a certain sense, as nothing, that is, that the mind ought never for a moment to be directed to them, but to the living God, and to the living God alone. I saw that such promises ought not to be of the value of one farthing so far as it regards thinking about them for help. Therefore, I asked the Lord, when, as usual, I was praying with my beloved wife about the work in my hands, that He would be pleased to take this whole matter about that promise completely out of my mind, and to help me not to value it in the least. Yes, I prayed to treat it as if it were not worth one farthing, but to keep my eyes directed only on God. I was enabled to do so. We had not yet finished praying when I received the following letter:

---

* Henry Craik, a Scotsman whom George Müller met in Teignmouth, shared pastoral duties with Müller at two chapels, Gideon and Bethesda, in Bristol.

May 5, 1845

Beloved Brother,

Are your bankers still Stuckey and Co. of Bristol, and are their bankers still Robarts and Co. of London? Please instruct me on this. If the case is so, please regard this as a letter to inform you that £70 will be paid to Robarts and Co. for Stuckey and Co. on your behalf. Apply this sum as the Lord may give you wisdom. I will not send the money to Robarts and Co. until I hear from you.

Ever affectionately yours.

Thus the Lord rewarded at once this determination to endeavor not to look in the least to that promise from a brother, but only to God. But this was not all. About two o'clock this afternoon, I received from the brother, who had more than forty days ago made that promise, £166 18s., as he this day received the money on the strength of which he had made the promise. Of this sum, £100 is to be used for the work in my hands, and the remainder for brother Craik's and my own personal expenses.

Faith Is from God

So that people would know that his faith was not a unique faith available only to him, Müller wrote in 1842,

I desire that all children of God who read these details may thereby be led to increased and more simple confidence in God for everything they may need under any circumstances. I trust that these many answers to prayer may encourage them to pray, particularly for the conversion of their friends and relatives, their own progress in grace and knowledge, the state of the saints whom they may know personally, the state of the church of God at large, and the success of the preaching of the Gospel. Especially I affectionately warn them against being led away by the tricks of Satan (see 2 Peter 3:17) to think that these things are unique to me, and that they cannot be enjoyed by all the children of God.

Although, as has been stated before, every believer is not called upon to establish orphanages or charities and trust in the Lord for the support of these institutions, yet all believers are called upon, in the simple confidence of faith, to cast all their burdens upon Him (Ps. 55:22). They are to trust in Him for everything (Ps. 37:5; Prov. 3:5), and not only to make everything a subject of prayer, but to expect answers to their petitions that they have asked according to His will and in the name of the Lord Jesus (Matt. 21:22; John 11:22).

Think not, dear reader, that I have the gift of faith, that is, the gift of which we read in 1 Corinthians 12:9, and which is mentioned along with *"gifts of healings"* (v. 9), *"the working of miracles"* (v. 10), and *"prophecy"* (v. 10), and that on that account, I am able to trust in the Lord. It is true that the faith that I am enabled to exercise is altogether God's own gift. It is true that He alone supports it, and that He alone can increase it. It is true that, moment by moment, I depend upon Him for it, and that, if I were only one moment left to myself, my faith would utterly fail; but it is not true that my faith is that gift of faith that is spoken of in 1 Corinthians 12:9, for the following reasons:

41

First, the faith that I am enabled to exercise with reference to the orphanages and my own temporal necessities is not that faith of which it is said in 1 Corinthians 13:2 (evidently alluding to the faith spoken of in 1 Corinthians 12:9), *"Though I have all faith, so that I could remove mountains, but have not love, I am nothing."* But it is the selfsame faith that is found in every believer, the growth of which I am most sensitive to within myself, for, little by little, it has been ever increasing throughout my Christian walk.

Second, this faith that is exercised in regard to the orphanages and my own temporal necessities shows itself in the same measure, for instance, concerning the following points: I have never been permitted to doubt since I accepted the Lord as my Savior that my sins are forgiven, that I am a child of God, that I am beloved of God, and that I will be finally saved, because I am enabled, by the grace of God, to exercise faith upon the Word of God and to believe what God says in those passages that settle these matters. (See 1 John 5:1; Galatians 3:26; Acts 10:43; Romans 10:9–10; John 3:16, among others.)

Further, when sometimes all has been dark, exceedingly dark, judging from natural appearances, with reference to my service among the saints, when I would have been overwhelmed in grief and despair if I had looked at things *"according to the outward appearance"*

(2 Cor. 10:7), at such times I have sought to encourage myself in God by laying hold in faith of His mighty power, His unchangeable love, and His infinite wisdom. I have said to myself, "God is able and willing to deliver me, if it is good for me; for it is written, *'He who did not spare His own Son, but delivered Him up for us all, how shall He not with Him also freely give us all things?'* (Rom. 8:32)." As I believed this promise through His grace, my soul was kept in peace.

Also, when in connection with the orphanages and day schools trials have come upon me that were far heavier than the lack of sufficient resources; when lying reports were spread that the orphans did not have enough to eat,* or that they were cruelly treated in other respects, and the like; or when other trials even greater, but which I cannot mention, have befallen me in connection with this work—and those at a time when I was nearly a thousand miles away from Bristol, and had to remain

---

* "There was not a great deal of variation in the food, but it was wholesome and regular. Porridge every morning for breakfast and meat for dinner on Mondays, Thursdays, and Fridays. On Tuesdays and Sundays, a dish of rice and raisins was commonplace. On Wednesdays and Saturdays, they were served broth with meat in it. Meat was either mutton—known to the children as 'Og'—or corned beef. The bread was known as 'Toke' because of the grace said at meals: *'We thank thee, Lord, for these tokens of thy love!'* Fresh fruit and eggs were in plentiful supply, and milk and water was the usual drink." From *The Bristol Miracle.* Used by permission from The George Müller Foundation.

absent week after week—at such times, my soul was stayed upon God. I believed His Word of promise, which was applicable to such cases. I poured out my soul before God and arose from my knees in peace, because the trouble that was in the soul was, in believing prayer, cast upon God; thus, I was kept in peace, even though I saw it to be the will of God to remain far away from the work.

Further, when I needed houses or fellow laborers for the orphans or for the day schools, I have been enabled to look to the Lord for everything and to trust in Him for help.

Dear reader, I may seem to boast, but, by the grace of God, I do not boast in speaking the way that I do. From my inmost soul, I ascribe the glory to God alone that He has enabled me to trust in Him, and that He has not allowed my confidence in Him to fail. But I thought it needful to make these remarks, lest anyone should think that my depending upon God was a particular gift given to me, which other saints have no right to look for, or lest it should be thought that my depending upon Him had only to do with the obtaining of money by prayer and faith.

By the grace of God, I desire that my faith in God might extend toward everything: the smallest of my own temporal and spiritual concerns, the least of the temporal and spiritual concerns of my family, the saints among whom I labor, the church at large, everything that has to do with the temporal and spiritual prosperity of the Scriptural Knowledge Institution, and so forth.

Dear reader, do not think that I have attained in faith (and how much less in other respects) to that degree to which I might and ought to attain; but thank God for the faith that He has given to me. Please pray that He will uphold and increase it.

Finally, once more, I remind you not to let Satan deceive you in making you think that you could not have the same faith, but that it is only for persons who are in a similar situation as I. When I lose something, such as a key, I ask the Lord to direct me to it, and I look for an answer to my prayer. When a person with whom I have made an appointment does not arrive according to the time agreed upon, and I begin to be inconvenienced by his lateness, I ask the Lord to be pleased to hasten him to me, and I look for an answer. When I do not understand a passage of the Word of God, I lift up my heart to the Lord and pray that He would be pleased, by His Holy Spirit, to instruct me, and I expect to be taught, though I do not set the time and the manner in which His answer will come. When I am going to minister from the Word, I seek help from the Lord, and while I, in the consciousness of my natural inability as well as my utter unworthiness, begin His service, I am not cast down, but of good cheer, because I look for His assistance. I believe that He, for His dear Son's sake, will help me. And thus in all of my temporal and spiritual concerns, I pray to the Lord and expect an answer to my requests.

May you not do the same, dear believing reader? Oh, I beseech you, do not think that I am an extraordinary believer, having privileges above any other of God's dear children, which they cannot have. Do not look on my way of acting as something that would not work for other believers. Give it a try! Stand still in the hour of trial, and you will see the help of God, if you trust in Him.

But there is so often a forsaking of the ways of the Lord in the hour of trial, and thus the food of faith, the means whereby our faith may be increased, is lost. This leads me to the following important point. You ask, How may I, a true believer, have my faith strengthened? Here is the answer: *"Every good gift and every perfect gift is from above, and comes down from the Father of lights, with whom there is no variation or shadow of turning"* (James 1:17). As the increase of faith is a good gift, it must come from God; therefore, He ought to be asked for this blessing. The following means, however, ought to be used:

First, carefully read the Word of God and meditate on it. Through reading the Word of God, and especially through meditation on the Word of God, the believer becomes more acquainted with the nature and character of God. Thus he sees more and more, besides His holiness and justice, what a kind, loving, gracious, merciful, mighty, wise, and faithful God He is. Therefore, in poverty, affliction of body, bereavement in his family, difficulty in his service, or lack of employment, he will rest upon the ability of God to help him, because he has not only learned from God's Word that He is of almighty power and infinite wisdom, but he has also seen instance upon instance in the Holy Scriptures in which His almighty power and infinite wisdom have been actually exercised in helping and delivering His people. He will rely upon the willingness of God to help him because he has not only learned from the Scriptures what a kind, good, merciful, gracious, and faithful being God is, but he has also seen in the Word of God how, in a great variety of instances, God has proved Himself to be so. And the consideration of this, if God has become known to us through prayer and meditation on His own Word, will lead us with a measure of confidence, in general at least, to rely upon Him. Thus the reading of the Word of God, together with meditation on it, will be one special means to strengthen our faith.

Second, with reference to the growth of every grace of the Spirit, it is of the utmost importance that we seek to maintain an upright heart and a good conscience; therefore, we should not knowingly or habitually indulge in those things that are contrary to the mind of God. So it is also particularly the case with reference to the growth in faith. How can I possibly continue to ask with faith in God concerning anything if I am habitually grieving Him and seeking to detract from the glory and honor of Him in whom I profess to trust, and upon whom I profess to depend? All my confidence toward God, all my leaning upon Him in the hour of trial, will be gone if I have a guilty conscience and do not seek to put away this guilty conscience, but continue to do the things that are contrary to the mind of God. And if, in any particular instance, I cannot trust in God because of a guilty conscience, then my faith is weakened by that instance of distrust. For with every fresh trial, faith either increases by my trusting God, and thus receiving His help, or it decreases by my not trusting Him. Then there is less and less power of looking simply and directly to Him, and a habit of self-dependence is born or encouraged. One or the other of these will always be the case in each particular instance. Either we trust in God, and in that case we do not trust in ourselves or in our fellowmen or in circumstances or in anything else; or we do trust in one or more of these, and in that case, we do not trust in God.

Third, if we desire our faith to be strengthened, we should not shrink from opportunities where our faith may be tried, and therefore, through the trials, be strengthened. In our natural state, we dislike dealing with God alone. Through our natural alienation from God, we shrink from Him, and from eternal realities. This tendency cleaves to us, more or less, even after our regeneration. Hence it is that, more or less, even as believers, we have the same shrinking from standing with God alone, from depending upon Him alone, or from looking to Him alone. Yet this is the very position in which we ought to be if we wish our faith to be strengthened. The more I am in a position to be tried in faith with reference to my body, my family, my service for the Lord, my business, and so on, the more I will have the opportunity of seeing God's help and deliverance. Every fresh instance in which He helps and delivers me will tend to increase my faith. On this account, therefore, the believer should not shrink from situations, positions, or circumstances in which his faith may be tried; instead, he should cheerfully embrace them as opportunities in which he may see the hand of God stretched out on his behalf to help and deliver him, and whereby he may thus have his faith strengthened.

The last important point for the strengthening of our faith is that we let God work for us when the hour of the trial of faith comes, and do not try to work a deliverance of our own. Wherever God has given faith, it has been given, among other reasons, for the very purpose of being tried.

Yes, however weak our faith may be, God will try it, but with this restriction: as in every way, He leads gently, gradually, and patiently, so also with reference to the trial of our faith. At first our faith will be tried very little in comparison with what it may be afterward, for God never lays more upon us than He is willing to enable us to bear (1 Cor. 10:13).

Now when the trial of faith comes, we are naturally inclined to distrust God and to trust instead in ourselves—or in our friends or our circumstances. We would rather achieve a deliverance of our own somehow or other than simply look to God and wait for His help. But if we do not patiently wait for God's help, if we seek a deliverance of our own, then at the next trial of our faith, it will be the same as before: we will once again be inclined to try to deliver ourselves. Thus, with every fresh instance of this kind, our faith will decrease; while on the contrary, if we were to *"stand still and see the salvation of the LORD"* (2 Chron. 20:17), to see His hand stretched out on our behalf, and to trust in Him alone, then our faith would be increased. With every new case in which the hand of God was stretched out on our behalf in the hour of the trial of our faith, our faith would be increased even more. If the believer, therefore, would have his faith strengthened, he must especially give time to God, who tries his faith in order to prove to His child, in the end, how willing He is to help and deliver him, the moment it is good for him.

Trials Can Strengthen Faith

In the early years of the Scriptural Knowledge Institution, Müller and his coworkers had to endure many severe trials of faith, as some of the following instances show. When writing of this period, George Müller said,

Though now (July 1845) for about seven years our funds have been so exhausted that it has been a rare case to have the means in hand to meet the necessities of more than one hundred persons for three days in a row, yet only once have I been tried in spirit. That was on September 18, 1838, when, for the first time, the Lord did not seem to pay attention to our prayers. But when He did send help, I saw that it was only for the trial of our faith, and not because He had forsaken the work, that we were brought so low. My soul was strengthened and encouraged, so that, since that time, I have not only not been allowed to distrust the Lord, but also not even been cast down when in the deepest poverty.

An Encouraging Gift

August 20, 1838. The £5 that I had received on August 18 had been given for housekeeping, so today I was penniless again. But my eyes looked up to the Lord. I gave myself to prayer this morning, knowing that I would need at least £13 this week, possibly as much as £20. Today I received £12 in answer to prayer from a lady who is staying at Clifton, whom I had never seen before. Loving Lord, grant that this may be a fresh encouragement to me.

A Solemn Crisis

Regarding one of the most difficult times of trial, Müller wrote,

September 10, 1838, Monday morning. No money had come in either on Saturday or yesterday. It appeared to me that it was now necessary to take some steps on account of our need, that is, to go to the orphanages, call the brothers and sisters together (who, except for Brother T——, had never been informed about the state of the funds), present the case to them, see how much money was needed for the present, tell them that amid this whole trial of faith, I still believed that God would help, and pray with them. I especially intended to go for the sake of telling them that no more articles must be purchased than we have the means to pay for. At the same time, I wanted them to know that the children should not go without nourishing food and necessary clothing. I would rather send them away at once than to have them go without their basic needs being met. I also intended to go for the sake of seeing whether there were still articles remaining that had been sent for the purpose of being sold, or whether there were any articles that were really not needed, so that we might turn them into money. I felt that the matter had now come to a solemn crisis. About half past nine, sixpence came in, which had been placed anonymously into the box at Gideon Chapel. This money seemed to me like an earnest, a pledge that God would have compassion and send more.

About ten, after I had returned from talking with brother Craik, to whom I had unburdened my heart again, while once more in prayer for help, a sister called who gave two sovereigns to my wife for the orphans. She stated that she had felt herself stirred up to come and that she had delayed too long in coming already. A few minutes later, when I went into the room where she was, she gave me two sovereigns more, all without knowing anything in the least about our need. Thus the Lord most mercifully has sent us a little help, to the great encouragement of my faith. A few minutes later, I was called on for money by the orphanage for infants, to which I sent £2. I also sent £1 0s. 6d. to the boys' orphanage, and £1 to the girls' orphanage.

A Precious Deliverance

It would have been easy for Müller to have had faith when the cupboards and bank account were full, but even during times of testing, he relied on the certainty of God's promises:

September 17, 1838. The trial still continues. It is now more and more trying, even to faith, as each day comes. Truly, the Lord has wise purposes in allowing us to call so long upon Him for help. But I am sure God will send help, if we can but wait. One of the laborers had had a little money come in, of which he gave 12s. 6d.; another worker gave 11s. 8d., which was all the money she had left. This amount, along with 17s. 6d., which partly had come in and partly was in hand, enabled us to pay what needed to be paid and to purchase provisions, so that nothing yet, in any way, has been lacking. This evening I was rather tried respecting the long delay of larger sums coming, but being led to go to the Scriptures for comfort, my soul was greatly refreshed. My faith again was strengthened by Psalm 34, so that I went very cheerfully to meet with my dear fellow laborers for prayer. I read the psalm to them and sought to cheer their hearts through the precious promises contained in it.

September 18. Brother T—— had 25s. in hand, and I had 3s. This £1 8s. enabled us to buy the meat and bread that were needed, a little tea for one of the houses, and milk for all. No more than this is needed. Thus the Lord has provided not only for this day, but for tomorrow as well, for there is bread on hand for two days. Now, however, we have come to an extreme situation. The funds are exhausted. The laborers, who had a little money, have given as long as they had any left. Now observe how the Lord helped us.

A lady from the neighborhood of London, who brought a parcel with money from her daughter, arrived four or five days ago in Bristol and took lodging next door to the boys' orphanage. This afternoon, she kindly brought me the money herself, amounting to £3 2s. 6d. We had been reduced so low as to be at the point of selling those things that could be spared, but this morning I had asked the Lord, if it might be, to prevent the necessity of our doing so. That the money had been so near the orphanages for several days without being given is a plain proof that it was from the beginning in the heart of God to help us. But because He delights in the prayers of His children, He had allowed us to pray so long. He also permitted our faith to be tried in order to make the answer so much the sweeter. It is indeed a precious deliverance. I burst out into loud praises and thanks the first moment I was alone, after I had received the money. I met with my fellow workers again this evening for prayer and praise; their hearts were visibly cheered. This money was divided this evening, and will comfortably provide for all that will be needed tomorrow.

Now to Him who is able to do exceedingly abundantly above all that we ask or think, according to the power that works in us, to Him be glory in the church by Christ Jesus to all generations, forever and ever. Amen.
—Ephesians 3:20–21

Chapter Two

The New Orphanages at Ashley Down

After a complaint was received in October 1845 that some of the inhabitants of Wilson Street were inconvenienced by the orphanages being located there, Müller decided, after much prayer and thoughtful consideration for his neighbors, to build an orphanage elsewhere. He wanted to be able to accommodate 300 children, plus have adequate property for them to exercise and play outdoors, so he began to ask the Lord for the means to go forward with this plan.

January 31, 1846. It is now eighty-nine days since I have been daily waiting upon God concerning the building of an orphanage. The time now seems to be near when the Lord will give us a piece of ground, and I told the brothers and sisters so this evening after our usual Saturday evening prayer meeting at the orphanages.

February 1. Today a poor widow sent ten shillings.

February 2. Today I heard of suitable and cheap land on Ashley Down.

February 3. Saw the land. It is the most desirable of all that I have seen. A sovereign was anonymously put in an orphan box at my house, as well as a piece of paper on which was written, "The New Orphanage."

February 4. This evening I called on the owner of the land on Ashley Down, about which I had heard on the 2nd, but he was not at home. As I, however, had been informed that I would find him at his place of business, I went there, but did not find him there either, since he had just left. I might have called again at his residence at a later hour, having been informed by one of the servants that he would be sure to be at home about eight o'clock, but I did not do so, judging that the hand of God was in my not finding him at either place. Therefore, I judged it best not to force the matter, but to *"let patience have its perfect work"* (James 1:4).

February 5. This morning, I saw the owner of the land. He told me that he awoke at three o'clock this morning and could not sleep again until five. All the time that he was lying awake, his mind was preoccupied with the piece of land, respecting the inquiry that had been made to him at my request for the building of an orphanage. He determined that if I applied for it, he would not only let me have it, but that he would charge only £120 per acre, instead of £200, the price that he had previously asked for it. How good the Lord is! The agreement was made this morning, and I purchased a field of nearly seven acres at £120 per acre. Observe the hand of God in my not finding the owner at home last evening! The Lord meant to speak to His servant first about this matter, during a sleepless night, and to lead him fully to decide before I had seen him.

The Rewards of Persistent Prayer

As God was faithful to answer, George Müller was faithful to keep on praying:

November 19, 1846. Now I am led more and more to persistently beseech the Lord to send me the means that are necessary in order that I may be able to begin the building. I do so because, first of all, it has been for some time publicly stated in print that some of the inhabitants of Wilson Street consider themselves inconvenienced by the orphanages being located on that street. I agree that they have some grounds for their complaints; therefore, I long to be able to remove the orphans from there as soon as possible.

Second, I become more and more convinced that it would greatly benefit the children, both physically and morally, with God's blessing, to be in such a position as they are intended to occupy when the new orphanage has been built.

Third, the number of very poor and destitute orphans who are waiting for admission is so great, and new applications are constantly being made.

Now while, by God's grace, I would not wish the building to be begun one single day sooner than is His will, and while I firmly believe that He will give me, in His own time, every shilling that I need, yet I also know that He delights in being earnestly asked and that He takes pleasure in the continuance in prayer. His teaching about persevering prayer may clearly be seen from the parable of the widow and the unjust judge. (See Luke 18:1–8.)

For these reasons, I gave myself again particularly to prayer last evening that the Lord would send means.

I was especially led to do so, in addition to the above reasons, because comparatively little had come in since the twenty-ninth of last month. This morning, between five and six o'clock, I prayed again, among other concerns, about the Building Fund. Then, I had a long season for the reading of the Word of God. In the course of my reading, I came to Mark 11:24, *"Therefore I say to you, whatever things you ask when you pray, believe that you receive them, and you will have them."* I have often felt and spoken about the importance of the truth contained in this passage, but this morning, I felt it again most particularly. Applying it to the new orphanage, I said to the Lord, "Lord, I believe that You will give me all I need for this work. I am sure that I will have all, because I believe that I receive in answer to my prayer." Thus, with a heart full of peace concerning this work, I went on to the rest of the eleventh chapter of Mark, and then to the next chapter.

After family prayer, I again had my usual season for prayer with regard to all the many parts of the work, and the various necessities thereof, asking blessings upon my fellow laborers, upon the circulation of Bibles and tracts, and upon the precious souls in the adult school, the Sunday schools, the six day schools, and the four orphanages. Amid all these many things, I again made my requests about means for the building.

And now observe: about five minutes after I had risen from my knees, a registered letter was given to me. It contained a check for £300, of which £280 are for the Building Fund, £10 for my own personal expenses, and £10 for brother Craik. May the Lord's holy name be praised for this precious encouragement by which the Building Fund is now increased to more than £6000.

The Joy of Answered Prayer

January 25, 1847. The season of the year is now approaching when building may be begun. Therefore, with increased earnestness, I have given myself to prayer, sincerely asking the Lord that He would be pleased to appear on our behalf and speedily send the remainder of the amount that is required. I have increasingly, of late, felt that the time is drawing near when the Lord will give me all that is needed for starting the construction of the building.

All the arguments that I have often brought before God, I brought again this morning before Him. It is now fourteen months and three weeks since, day by day, I have uttered my petitions to God on behalf of this work. I rose from my knees this morning in full confidence, not only that God could, but also would, send the means, and that He would do it soon. Never, during all these fourteen months and weeks, have I had the least doubt that I would have all that is required.

And now, dear believing reader, rejoice and praise God with me. About an hour after I had prayed, the sum of two thousand pounds was given to me for the building. Thus I have received altogether £9,285 3s. 9 ½ d. toward this work. I cannot describe the joy I had in God when I received this donation. It must be known from experience in order to be felt. For four hundred forty-seven days, I have had to wait upon God day by day before the sum reached the above amount. How great is the blessing that the soul obtains by trusting in God, and by waiting patiently! Is it not clear how precious it is to carry on God's work in this way, even with regard to the obtaining of means?

The total amount that came in for the Building Fund was £15,784 18s. 10d.

Waiting Brings Its Reward

March 12, 1862. It was in November 1850 that I began to think about enlarging the orphan work from 300 orphans to 1000, and subsequently to 1150. It was in June 1851 that my purpose became known, after I had kept it secret for more than seven months while day by day praying about it. From the end of November 1850, to this day, March 12, 1862, not one single day has been allowed to pass without the contemplated enlargement being brought before God in prayer, generally more than once a day. But only now, this day, the new third orphanage was completed enough so that it could be opened. Observe then, first, esteemed reader, how long it may be before a full answer to our prayers, even to thousands and tens of thousands of prayers, is granted—yes, even though those prayers may be believing prayers, earnest prayers, offered up in the name of the Lord Jesus, and even though we may only for the sake of the honor of our Lord desire the answer. I did, by the grace of God, without the least doubt and wavering, look for more than eleven years for the full answer, and I sought only the glory of God in this matter.

God Is Always on Time

As in the case of the second orphanage, so also in the case of the third orphanage, I had daily prayed for the needed helpers and assistants for the various departments. Before a stone was laid, I began to pray for workers, and, as the building progressed, I continued day by day to bring this matter before God. I felt assured that, as in everything else, so in this specific need also, God would graciously be pleased to appear on our behalf and help us, since the whole work is intended for His honor and glory.

At last the time was near when the house could be opened, and the time therefore was near when the applications, which had been made in writing during more than two years previously, should be considered for the filling of the various posts. It now, however, was found that, while there had been about fifty applications made for the various situations, some places could not be filled, because either the individuals who had applied for them were married, or were, upon examination, found unsuitable. This was no small trial of faith, for day by day, for years, I had asked God to help me in this specific concern, even as He had done in the case of the second new orphanage. I had also expected help, confidently expected help, and yet now, when help seemed needed, it was lacking. What was now to be done, dear reader? Would it have been right to charge God with unfaithfulness? Would it have been right to distrust Him? Would it have been right to say, "It is useless to pray"? By no means.

On the contrary, this is what I did. I thanked God for all the help He had given me in connection with the whole expansion of the ministry. I thanked Him for enabling me to overcome so many and such great difficulties. I thanked Him for the helpers He had given me for the second new orphanage. I also thanked Him for the helpers He had given me already for the third new orphanage; and instead of distrusting God, I looked upon this delay of the full answer to prayer only as a trial of faith. Instead of praying once a day with my dear wife about this matter, as we had been doing day by day for years, I determined that we should now meet three times daily to bring this request before God. I also brought the matter before the whole staff of my helpers in the work, requesting their prayers. Thus I have now continued for about four months longer in prayer, day by day calling upon God three times on account of this need, and the result has been that one helper after the other has been given, without the help coming too late or the work getting into confusion or the reception of the children being hindered. I am fully assured that the few who are yet needed will also be found, when they are really required.

Prayer and Patience Remove Obstacles

After receiving an additional £5000 for the Building Fund, Müller related the following incidents in connection with the purchase of the land for the fourth and fifth orphanages:

I had now, through all that had come in since May 26, 1864, more than £27,000 in hand. I had patiently waited for God's time. I had determined to do nothing until I had the full half of the sum needed for the two houses. But now, having more than two thousand pounds beyond the half, I felt, after again seeking counsel from God, quite happy in taking steps for the purchase of land.

For years, my eyes had been directed to a beautiful piece of land, only separated by the turnpike road from the ground on which the third new orphanage is erected. The land is about eighteen acres, with a small house and outhouses built on one end of the property. Hundreds of times I had prayed, within the last years, that God for Jesus' sake would count me worthy to be allowed to erect two more orphanages on this ground. Hundreds of times I had with a prayerful eye looked on this land, yes, as it were, saturated it with my prayers.

I might have bought it years ago, but that would have been going before the Lord. I had money enough in hand to have paid for it years ago, but I desired patiently, submissively, to wait on God's own time, and for Him to mark it clearly and distinctly that His time had come, and that I was taking the step according to His will. I knew that whatever I might apparently accomplish, if the work were mine and not the Lord's, I could expect no blessing. But now the Lord's mind was clearly and distinctly made manifest. I had enough money in hand to pay for the land and to build one house; therefore, I went forward after having still asked the Lord for guidance, and being assured that it was His will that I should take active steps.

The first thing I did was to see the agent who acted for the owner of the land and to ask him whether the land was for sale. He replied that it was, but that it was leased until March 25, 1867. He said that he would write for the price. Here a great difficulty at once presented itself: that the land was leased for two years and four months longer, while it appeared desirable that I should be able to take possession of it in about six months, that is to say, as soon as the conveyance could be made out, the plans be readied for the fourth new orphanage, and arrangements be made with contractors. But I was not discouraged by this difficulty, for I expected, through prayer, to make happy and satisfactory arrangements with the tenant, being willing to give him a fair compensation for leaving before his time had expired.

But before I had time to see about this matter, two other great difficulties presented themselves: one was that the owner asked £7,000 for the land, which I judged to be considerably more than its value; and the other was that I heard that the Bristol Waterworks Company intended to make an additional reservoir for its water on this very land, and to get an Act of Parliament passed to that effect.

Pause here for a few moments, dear reader. You have seen how the Lord brought me so far with regard to monetary means that I felt warranted to go forward. I may further add that I was brought to this point as the result of praying thousands of times regarding this objective, and that there were, also, many hundreds of children waiting for admission. Yet after the Lord Himself so manifestly had appeared on our behalf by the donation of £5000, He allowed this apparent death-blow to come upon the whole endeavor. But thus I have found it hundreds of times since I have known the Lord that the difficulties, which He is pleased to allow to arise, are only permitted under such circumstances for the exercise of our faith and patience. More prayer, more patience, and the exercise of faith will remove the difficulties.

Now, since I knew the Lord, these difficulties were not insurmountable to me, for I put my trust in Him, according to His Word:

The LORD also will be a refuge for the oppressed, a refuge in times of trouble. And those who know Your name will put their trust in You; for You, LORD, have not forsaken those who seek You.

(Ps. 9:9–10)

I gave myself, therefore, earnestly to prayer concerning these three special difficulties that had arisen regarding the land. I prayed several times daily about the matter, and used the following means:

First, I saw the Acting Committee of the Directors of the Bristol Waterworks Company regarding their intended reservoir on the land that I was about to purchase, and stated to them what I had seen in print concerning their intentions. They courteously stated to me that only a small portion of the land would be required, not enough to interfere with my purpose; and that, if it could be avoided, even this small portion would not be taken.

Second, this matter being settled, I now saw the tenant, after many prayers; for I desired, as a Christian, that if this land were bought, it should be done under amicable circumstances with regard to him. At the first interview, I stated my intentions to him, at the same time expressing my desire that the matter should be settled pleasantly with regard to himself. He said that he would consider the matter and desired a few days for that purpose. After a week I saw him again, and he then kindly stated that, as the land was wanted for such a purpose, he would not stand in the way, but that, as he had laid out a good deal on the house and land, he expected a compensation for leaving it before his time was up. As I, of course, was quite willing to give a fair and reasonable compensation, I considered this a very precious answer to prayer.

Next, I now entered upon the third difficulty, the price of the land. I knew well how much the land was worth to us for the building of another orphanage, but its value for our purposes was not the market value. I gave myself, therefore, day by day to prayer, that the Lord would constrain the owner to accept a considerably lower sum than he had asked. I also pointed out to the owner why it was not worth as much as he asked. At last he consented to take £5,500 instead of £7,000, and I accepted the offer. I knew that because the land was level, we would save a considerable sum for the two houses, and that because the new sewer, which only a few months before had been completed, ran along under the turnpike road near the field, we would be considerably benefited. In addition to these two points, I had to take into account that we could have gas from Bristol, as we do in the three houses already in operation.

And last, the most important point of all was the nearness of this piece of land to the other three houses, so that all could easily be under the same direction and supervision. In fact, no other piece of land, near or far, could present so many advantages to us as this spot, which the Lord had so very kindly given to us.

Now that everything was settled, I proceeded to have the land conveyed to the same trustees who stood trustees for the first three new orphanages. I have minutely dwelt on these matters for the encouragement of the reader, that he may not be discouraged by difficulties, however great and many and varied, but give himself to prayer, trusting in the Lord for help, yes, expecting help, which, in God's own time and way, He will surely grant.

God Is Trustworthy

March 5, 1874. Both houses, numbers four and five, have now been in operation for years, number four since November 1868, and number five since the beginning of 1870. More than 1,200 orphans have been already received into them, and month after month, more are received as the orphans are sent out from the homes as apprentices or servants. Moreover, all the expenses in connection with their being built and furnished were met to the full as the demands arose. After all had been paid, a balance of several thousand pounds was left, which is being used for keeping the houses in repair.

See, esteemed reader, how abundantly God answered our prayers, and how plain it is that we were not mistaken, after we had patiently and prayerfully sought to ascertain His will. Be encouraged, therefore, yet further and further to confide in the living God.

Whatever you ask in My name, that I will do,
that the Father may be glorified in the Son.
If you ask anything in My name, I will do it.
—John 14:13–14

Chapter Three

Precious Answers to Prayer

George Müller said that he knew of over fifty thousand specific answers to his prayers. Here are some that he recorded in the several volumes of his *Narrative:*

An Artist Shares His Blessing

April 30, 1859. I received the following letter from a considerable distance:

My dear Christian brother,

I am the husband of Mrs. ——, who sends you by this post the two-sovereign piece. How can we better dispose of this relic of affectionate remembrance than by depositing it in the bank of Christ? He always pays the best interest and never fails.

Now, my best and spiritual counselor, I cannot express to you the exceeding great joy I feel in relating what follows: I am an artist, a poor artist, a landscape painter. About two weeks ago, I sent a picture to Bristol for exhibition, just as I finished your book that was lent to us. I most humbly and earnestly prayed to God to enable me, by the sale of my Bristol picture, to have the blessed privilege of sending you half the proceeds. The price of the picture is £20. Now mark. Immediately, as soon as the exhibition opened, God, in His mercy, mindful of my prayer, sent me a purchaser. I have exhibited in Bristol before, but never sold a picture. Oh, my dear friend, my very heart leaps for joy! I have never been so near God before. Through your instrumentality, I have been enabled to draw nearer to God, with more earnestness, more faith, and more holy desires.

This is the first return God has blessed me with for the whole of my last year's labors. What a blessing to have it so returned!

Oh, with what joy I read your book! The picture I speak of is now being exhibited in the academy of arts at Clifton. I cannot pay you until the close of the exhibition, as I will not be paid until then.

I have had thousands of letters like this one during the last forty years.

The North Wind Changed into a South Wind

It was toward the end of November 1857 when I was most unexpectedly informed that the boiler of our heating apparatus at the first new orphanage leaked very considerably. It was impossible for us to go through the winter with the boiler in such a condition.

Our heating apparatus consists of a large cylinder boiler, inside of which the fire is kept, and with which the water pipes that warm the rooms are connected. Hot air is also connected to this apparatus. The boiler had been considered suited for the work of the winter. To suspect that it was worn out and not to have done anything toward replacing it with a new one, and to have said, "I will trust God to take care of it," would have been careless presumption—not faith in God. It would have been exercising a counterfeit faith.

The boiler is entirely surrounded by brickwork; its state, therefore, could not be known without taking down the brick. If done needlessly, this task would be rather injurious to the boiler. Since for eight winters we had had no difficulty in this way, we had not anticipated it now. But suddenly, and most unexpectedly, at the beginning of winter, this difficulty occurred. What then was to be done?

I felt deeply concerned for the children, especially the younger infants, not wanting them to suffer because of a lack of heat. But how were we to obtain warmth? The introduction of a new boiler would, in all probability, take many weeks. Repairing the boiler was a questionable matter because of the severity of the leak. Nothing could really be decided until the brick chamber in which it was enclosed, was, at least in part, removed; but, as far as we could judge, that would take days. What was to be done in the meantime to find warm rooms for three hundred children?

It naturally occurred to me to introduce temporary gas stoves, but on further weighing the matter, it was found that we would be unable to heat our very large rooms with gas, unless we had many stoves. We could not use this solution since we did not have a sufficient quantity of gas to spare from our lighting apparatus. Moreover, for each of these stoves, we needed a small chimney to carry off the impure air. This mode of heating, therefore, though applicable to a hall, a staircase, or a shop, would not suit our purpose.

I also thought of the temporary introduction of Arnott's stoves, but they would have been unsuitable, requiring long chimneys (since they would have been temporary) to go out of the windows. Because of the uncertainty of their providing a solution to our problem, and the fact that they would disfigure the rooms, I was led to give up this plan also. But what was to be done? I would gladly have paid £100 if thereby the difficulty could have been overcome, and the children would not have been caused to suffer from being in cold rooms. At last I determined to fall entirely into the hands of God, who is very merciful and of tender compassion. I decided to have the brick chamber opened in order to see the extent of the damage and whether the boiler might be repaired so as to carry us through the winter.

The day was set when the workmen were to come, and all the necessary arrangements were made. The fire, of course, had to be put out while the repairs were going on. But now see. After the day was set for the repairs, a bleak north wind set in. It began to blow either on the Thursday or Friday before the Wednesday afternoon when the fire was to be put out. Then came the first really cold weather, which we had in the beginning of that winter, during the first days of December. What was to be done? The repairs could not be put off. I asked the Lord for two things, namely, that He would be pleased to change the north wind into a south wind, and that He would give to each workman *"a mind to work."* I remembered how much Nehemiah accomplished in fifty-two days while building the walls of Jerusalem, because *"the people had a mind to work"* (Neh. 4:6).

Well, the memorable day came. The evening before, the bleak north wind still blew, but, on Wednesday, the south wind blew—exactly as I had prayed! The weather was so mild that no fire was needed. The brickwork was removed, the leak was discovered very quickly, and the boilermakers began the repairs in good earnest. About half past eight in the evening, when I was going home, I was informed at the lodge that the acting manager of the firm, from which the boilermakers came, had arrived to see how the work was going and if he could in any way speed the matter.

Immediately, I went to the cellar to see if he could expedite the business. I spoke to the manager of my concern about keeping the children warm, and he said, so that his workers could hear, "The men will work late this evening and come very early again tomorrow."

"We would rather, sir," said the leader, "work all night." Then I remembered the second part of my prayer, that God would give each man *"a mind to work."* Thus it was that by morning, the repair was accomplished, the leak was stopped, though with great difficulty, and within about thirty hours, the brickwork was up again, and the fire was lit in the boiler. All the time, the south wind blew mildly, so that there was not the least need of a fire. Here, then, is one of our difficulties that was overcome by prayer and faith.

Conversion of the Orphans

Although George Müller wanted the orphanages to stand as "visible proof" of the reality and faithfulness of God, the spiritual needs of the orphans were always a part of his earnest petitions to God. He sought God not only for their physical and emotional well-being, but also for their eternal salvation.

May 26, 1860. Day after day, year after year, by the help of God, we labor in prayer for the spiritual benefit of the orphans under our care. Our supplications, which have been for twenty-four years brought before the Lord concerning them, have been abundantly answered. Throughout the years, we have witnessed the conversion of hundreds from among them. We have also had repeated seasons in which, within a short time, or even all at once, many of the orphans were converted.

We had such a time about three years ago, when, within a few days, about sixty were brought to believe in the Lord Jesus. Such seasons we have had again twice during the past year. The first was in July 1859, when the Spirit of God worked mightily in one school of 120 girls, so that very many, yes more than one-half, were brought under deep concern about the salvation of their souls. This work, moreover, was not a mere momentary excitement, but, after more than eleven months have elapsed, there are thirty-one concerning whom there is full confidence as to their conversion, and thirty-two of whom there is likewise a considerable measure of confidence. There are 63 out of the 120 orphans in that one school who are considered to have been converted in July 1859. This blessed and mighty work of the Holy Spirit cannot be traced to any particular cause. It was, however, a most precious answer to prayer. As such, we look upon it and are encouraged by it to further waiting upon God.

The second season of the mighty working of the Holy Spirit among the orphans during the past year was at the end of January and the beginning of February 1860. The details of it are of the deepest interest, but I must content myself by stating that this great work of the Spirit of God began among the younger class of the children under our care, little girls of about six, seven, eight, and nine years of age. It then extended to the older girls, and then to the boys, so that within about ten days, more than two hundred of the orphans were stirred up to be concerned about their souls.

In many instances, they found peace immediately, through faith in our Lord Jesus. They at once requested to be allowed to hold prayer meetings among themselves, and they have had these meetings ever since. Many of them also showed a concern about the salvation of their companions and relatives, and spoke or wrote to them about the way to be saved.

Apprenticing the Orphans

In the early part of the summer of 1862, it was found that we had several boys who were ready to be apprenticed, but there were no applications made by masters for apprentices. As all our boys are invariably sent out as indoor apprentices, this was no small difficulty. We not only look for Christian masters, but also consider their businesses, and examine whether they are suitable. The master must also be willing to receive the apprentice into his own family. Under these circumstances, we again gave ourselves to prayer, as we had done for more than twenty years before concerning this thing. Instead of advertising, which, in all probability, would only have brought before us masters who desired apprentices for the sake of the premium, we looked to God to provide. We remembered how good the Lord had been to us in having helped us hundreds of times before in this very matter.

Some weeks passed, but the difficulty remained. We continued, however, in prayer, and then one application was made, and then another; and since we first began to pray about this matter last summer, we have been able to send out a total of eighteen boys up to May 26, 1863. The difficulty was thus again entirely overcome by prayer, as every one of the boys whom it was desirable to send out has been placed with a good family.

Sickness at the Orphanage

Disease was one of the most difficult challenges George Müller encountered in running the orphanages. Outbreaks of cholera and smallpox were not uncommon, due to the poor sanitary conditions of the times. Open sewers, unclean drinking water, uncollected garbage piled in the streets, and no system for removing the dead all contributed to a high death rate and the rapid spread of diseases. Among his many prayers for the children, George Müller prayed for their good health. At times, sickness visited the houses. Regarding one of these times, Müller wrote,

During the summer and autumn of 1866, we had an outbreak of the measles at all three orphanages. After they had made their appearance, our specific prayer was that there might not be too many children ill at one time with this disease, so that our accommodations in the infirmary rooms or otherwise might be sufficient. This prayer was answered completely. Although we had at the first new orphanage no less than 83 cases, in the second house 111 cases altogether, and in the third house 68 cases, yet God was graciously pleased to listen to our supplications. When our spare rooms were filled with sick children, He held back the spread of the measles until a sufficient number were restored, so as to make room for others who became ill.

We further prayed that the children who were taken ill with the measles might be safely brought through and not die. Thus it was. We had the full answer to our prayers, for though 262 children altogether had the measles, not one of them died.

Finally, we prayed that no physical consequences would follow this disease, as is so often the case; this answer, too, was granted. All the 262 children not only recovered, but also did well afterward. I gratefully record this significant mercy and blessing of God, and this full and precious answer to prayer, to the honor of His name.

Help for Needy Brothers

The end of the year (1863) was now at hand, and, in winding up the accounts, it was my earnest desire to do once more all I could in sending help to needy laborers in the Gospel; therefore, I went through the list, writing beside the various names of those to whom I had not already recently sent money, what amount it appeared desirable to send. When these sums were added together, I found that the total was £476, but £280 was all that I had on hand. Therefore, I wrote a check for £280. Although I would have gladly sent £476, I felt thankful, at the same time, that I had this amount available for these brothers.

Having written the check as the last item of the day, it was time for my usual season of prayer for the many things that I daily, by the help of God, bring before Him. Once again, I brought the case of these preachers of the Gospel before the Lord. I asked that He would even now be pleased to give me yet a considerable sum for them, though there remained but three days before the close of our year.

This being done, I went home about nine o'clock in the evening and found there had arrived from a great distance £100 for missions, with £100 left at my disposal, and £5 for myself. I took, therefore, the whole £200 for missions, and thus had £480 in hand to meet the £476 that I desired for this purpose. Those who know the blessedness of really trusting in God, and receiving help from Him, as in this case, in answer to prayer, will be able to enter into the spiritual enjoyment I had in the reception of that donation. The answer to prayer was granted, and with that answer came the great enjoyment of gladdening the hearts of many devoted servants of Christ.

The Heart's Desire Fulfilled

September 30, 1869. From Yorkshire came £50. Also £1000 was received today for the Lord's work in China. It is especially to be noticed about this donation that for months it had been my earnest desire to do more than ever for the mission work in China,[*] and I had already taken steps to carry out this desire when

---

[*] In the early 1870s, Müller sent approximately £10,000 pounds annually to support nearly two hundred missionaries, including Hudson Taylor and the work of the China Inland Mission.

this donation of £1000 came to hand. This precious answer to prayer for means should be a particular encouragement to all who are engaged in the Lord's work, and who may need the funds to carry it on. It proves afresh that, if our work is His work, and we honor Him by waiting upon and looking to Him for resources, He will surely, in His own time and way, supply them.

The Benefits of Answered Prayer

The joy that answers to prayer give cannot be described, and the impetus that they afford to the spiritual life is exceedingly great. I desire the experience of this happiness for all my Christian readers. If you *"believe on the Lord Jesus Christ"* (Acts 16:31) for the salvation of your soul, if you *"walk uprightly"* (Ps. 84:11) and do not *"regard iniquity in* [your] *heart"* (Ps. 66:18), if you continue to *"wait patiently"* (Ps. 37:7) and believe in God (Heb. 11:6), then answers will surely be given to your prayers. You may not be called upon to serve the Lord in the way this writer has been called; therefore, you may never have answers to prayer in regard to the things that are recorded here. But in your various circumstances, your family, your business, your profession, your church position, your labor for the Lord, and so on, you may have answers as specific as any that are recorded here.

The Great Need

Should these words, however, be read by any who are not believers in the Lord Jesus, but who are going on in the carelessness or self-righteousness of their unrenewed hearts, then I would affectionately and solemnly beseech such to first of all *"be reconciled to God"* (2 Cor. 5:20) by faith in the Lord Jesus. You are sinners. You deserve punishment. If you do not see this truth, then ask God to show it to you. Let this now be your first and specific prayer. Ask God to enlighten you not merely concerning your natural state, but also especially to reveal the Lord Jesus to your heart.

God sent Jesus so that He might bear the punishment due to us guilty sinners. God accepts the obedience and sufferings of the Lord Jesus in place of those who depend upon Him for the salvation of their souls. The moment a sinner believes in the Lord Jesus, he obtains the forgiveness of all his sins. When he is reconciled to God by faith in the Lord Jesus, and has obtained forgiveness for his sins, he has boldness to enter into the presence of God and to make his requests known to Him (Heb. 4:16).

The more he is enabled to realize that his sins are forgiven, and that God, for Christ's sake, is well pleased with those who believe in Him, the more ready he will be to come with all his needs, both temporal and spiritual, to his heavenly Father, so that He may supply them. But as long as the consciousness of unpardoned guilt remains, he will be kept at a distance from God, especially as it regards prayer. Therefore, dear reader, if you are an unforgiven sinner, let your first prayer be that God would be pleased to reveal to your heart the Lord Jesus, His beloved Son.

A Double Answer

July 25, 1865. From the neighborhood of London £100 was received along with the following letter:

My dear sir,

I believe that it is through the Lord's actions upon me that I enclose a check for you from the Bank of England, Western Branch, for £100. I hope that your affairs are going well.

Yours in the Lord.

This Christian gentleman, whom I have never seen, and who is engaged in a very large business in London, had several times before sent me a similar sum. A day or two before I received this last kind donation, I had asked the Lord if He would be pleased to influence the heart of this donor to help me again, which I had never done before regarding him. Thus I had a double answer to prayer, in that not only money came in, but money from him.

The reader will now see the meaning in the donor's letter, when he wrote, "I believe that it is through the Lord's actions upon me that I enclose a check for you." Truly it was the Lord who acted upon this gentleman, spurring him to send me this sum. Perhaps the reader may think that in acknowledging the receipt of the donation, I wrote to the donor what I have here stated. I did not. My reason for not doing so was lest he should have thought I was in particular need, and might have been influenced then to send more.

In truly knowing the Lord, in really relying upon Him and upon Him alone, there is no need of giving hints directly or indirectly, whereby individuals may be further induced to help. I could have written to the donor that I needed a considerable sum day by day for the current expenses for the various purposes of the Institution (as was indeed the case). I also might have truthfully told him, at that time, that I yet needed about twenty thousand pounds to enable me to meet all the expenses connected with the contemplated enlargement of the orphan work.

But my practice is never to allude to any of these things in my correspondence with donors. When the Report is published, everyone can see, who has a desire to see, how matters stand; thus, I leave things in the hands of God to speak for us to the hearts of His stewards. And this He does. Truly, we do not wait on God in vain!

Christians in Business

January 1, 1869. From Scotland £50 arrived for missions, £25 for the circulation of the Holy Scriptures, and £25 for the circulation of tracts. We also received from a considerable distance £10 for these purposes, with £10 for the orphans.

About this latter donation, I make a few remarks. At the early part of 1868, a Christian man wrote to me for advice in his difficult business affairs. His letter showed that he had a desire to walk in the ways of the Lord, and to carry on his business to the glory of God, but his circumstances were of the most trying character. I therefore wrote to him to come to Bristol so that I might be able to advise him. Accordingly, he undertook the long journey, and I had an interview with him, through which I saw his most trying position.

Having fully conversed with him, I gave him the following counsel:

First, he should, day by day, expressly for the purpose of prayer, retreat with his Christian

84

wife, so that they might in a unified spirit spread their business difficulties before God, and do this, if possible, twice a day.

Second, he should watch for answers to his prayers, and expect that God would help him.

Third, he should avoid all business fraud, such as advertising for sale two or three articles marked below cost price, for the sake of attracting customers, because of its being an unbecoming practice for a disciple of the Lord Jesus to use such crafty methods; and that, if he did so, he could not count on the blessing of God.

Next, I advised him further to set apart, out of his profits, week by week, a certain portion for the work of God, whether his income was much or little, and use this income faithfully for the Lord.

Last, I asked him to let me know, month after month, how the Lord dealt with him.

The reader will be interested to learn that from that time, the Lord was pleased to prosper the business of this dear Christian brother, so that his returns from March 1, 1868, to March 1, 1869, were £9,138 13s. 5d., while during the same period the previous year they had been only £6,609 18s. 3d., making a total of £2,528 15s. 2d. more than the year before.

When he sent me the donation referred to above, he also wrote that he had been enabled to put aside during the previous year £123 13s. 3d. for the work of God or the needs of the poor. I have so fully dwelt on this topic because Christians in business may be benefited by this lesson.

Revival in the Orphanages

In giving the statistics of the previous year (1871–72), I referred already to the great spiritual blessing that it pleased the Lord to grant to the orphan work at the end of that year and the beginning of this one; but, as this is so deeply important a subject, I enter somewhat further and more fully into it here.

It was stated before that the spiritual condition of the orphans generally brought great sorrow to our hearts, because there were so few among them who were in earnest about their souls and resting on the atoning death of the Lord Jesus for salvation. Our sorrow led us to lay it on the whole staff of assistants, matrons, and teachers to seek earnestly for the Lord's blessing on the souls of the children. This was done in our united prayer meetings, and, I have reason to believe, in secret sessions of prayer as well.

In the year 1872, in answer to and as a result of our private and united prayers, there were more believers by far among the orphans than ever. On January 8, 1872, the Lord began to work among them, and this work continued more or less afterward. In the third new orphanage, it showed itself least, until it pleased the Lord to lay His hand heavily on that house by an outbreak of smallpox. From that time, the working of the Holy Spirit was felt in that house also, particularly in one department.

At the end of July 1872, I received the statements of all the matrons and teachers in the five houses, who reported to me that, after careful observation and conversation, they had good reason to believe that 729 of the orphans then under our care were believers in the Lord Jesus. This number of believing orphans was by far greater than we had ever had before, for which we adore and praise the Lord! See how the Lord overruled the great trial caused by smallpox and turned it into a great blessing! See also, how, after so low a state, comparatively, which led us to earnest prayer, the working of the Holy Spirit was more manifest than ever!

Müller's Mission Tours

In the year 1875, when seventy years of age, Müller began his missionary tours. During the next seventeen years, he preached to three million people in forty-two countries of the world.

Writing about his missionary journeys, Müller said,

On August 8, 1882, we began our ninth missionary tour. The first place at which I preached was Weymouth, where I spoke in public four times. From Weymouth we went, by way of Calais and Brussels, to Düsseldorf on the Rhine, where I had preached many times six years before. During this visit, I spoke in public eight times. Regarding my stay at Düsseldorf, for the encouragement of the reader, I relate the following circumstance:

During our first visit to that city, in the year 1876, a godly missionary came to me one day, greatly tried because he had six sons for whose conversion he had been praying many years, but who remained unconcerned about their souls. He desired for me to tell him what to do. My reply was, "Continue to pray for your sons, expect an answer to your prayers, and you will have to praise God."

Now, when after six years I was again in the same city, this dear man came to me and said he was surprised he had not seen before what he ought to do, and that he had resolved to take my advice and more earnestly than ever give himself to prayer. Two months after he saw me, five of his six sons were converted within eight days, and have for six years now walked in the ways of the Lord. He had hope that the sixth son was beginning to be concerned about his state before God as well.

May the Christian reader be encouraged by this, should his prayers not at once be answered; instead of ceasing to pray, he should wait upon God all the more earnestly and perseveringly, and expect answers to his petitions.

Willing to Serve

The Bristol Chapel, where Müller pastored, was privileged to set an example to the church of God by the way in which foreign missionaries, who are so greatly needed, were sent forth in answer to prayer. Müller wrote in his *Narrative,*

I also mention here that during the eight years previous to my going to Germany to labor there, it had been laid on my heart, and on the hearts of some other brothers among us, to ask the Lord if He would be pleased to honor us, as a body of believers, by calling forth from our midst, brothers who would carry the truth into foreign lands. But this prayer seemed to remain unanswered.

After eight years, however, the time had come when the Lord was about to answer it, and I, on whose heart particularly this matter had been laid, was to be the first to carry forth the truth from among us. (For a brief period in 1838, George returned to the land of his childhood.) About that very time, the Lord called our dear brother and sister Barrington from among us, to go to Demerara, to labor there in connection with our esteemed brother Strong. He also called our dear brother and sister Espenett to go to Switzerland. These dear friends left shortly after I had gone to Germany.

But this was not all. Our much valued brother Mordal, who had commended himself to the saints by his unwearied faithful service among us for twelve years, had—from August 31, 1843, the day on which brothers Strong and Barrington sailed from Bristol for Demerara—his mind and heart led to missionary service there. Thus, he went out from among us eleven months later. He, together with myself, had had it particularly laid upon his heart, during the eight years previously, to ask the Lord again and again to call laborers from among us for foreign service. Of all persons, he, the father of a large family, and about fifty years of age, seemed the least likely to be called to that work, but God did call him. He went and labored a little while in Demerara; then, on January 9, 1845, the Lord took him to his rest.

When we ask God for a thing, such as would He be pleased to raise up laborers for His harvest, or send means for the carrying on of His work, the honest questions to be put to our hearts should be these: Am I willing to go if He should call me? Am I willing to give according to my ability? For we may be the very persons whom the Lord will call for the work, or whose means He may wish to employ.

The Divine Plan

In the 1896 Report of the Scriptural Knowledge Institution for Home and Abroad, Müller showed how greatly this body of believers had been honored by God.

From our own midst, as a church, sixty brothers and sisters have gone forth to foreign fields of labor; some have finished their work on earth, but there are still about forty engaged in this precious service.

Why should not the great and crying need for workers in Asia, Africa, and other parts of the world be met by thousands of churches in Europe and America following this divine plan of praying for *"the Lord of the harvest to send out laborers into His harvest"* (Luke 10:2) from among them?

Surely they may expect God to answer their prayers as He did the prayers of the Bristol Chapel. Look what has been done in China by the faithful use of God's method! We quote Hudson Taylor's[*] words as given in *China's Millions* for July 1897:

For the obtaining of fellow workers, we took the Master's direction, "Pray the Lord of the harvest." As for the first five before the Mission was formed, so for the twenty-four for whom we first asked for the CIM [China Inland

---

[*] Hudson Taylor (1832–1905) was a pioneer missionary to China.

Mission], for further reinforcements when they were needed, for the seventy in three years, for the hundred in one year, and for further additions from time to time, we have ever relied on this plan. Is it possible that in any other way such a band of workers from nearly every denomination, and from many lands, could have been gathered and kept together for thirty years with no other bond except that which the call of God and the love of God has proved—a band now numbering over seven hundred men and women, aided by more than five hundred native workers?

The Beginning of the 1859 Revival

In November 1856, a young Irishman, James McQuilken, was brought to the knowledge of the Lord. Soon after his conversion, he saw my *Narrative* advertised. He had a great desire to read it and procured it accordingly, about January 1857. God blessed it greatly to his soul, especially in showing to him what could be obtained by prayer. He said to himself something like this: "See what Mr. Müller obtains simply by prayer. Thus I may obtain blessing by prayer."

He now set himself to pray that the Lord would give him a spiritual companion, one who knew the Lord. Soon after, he became acquainted with a young man who was a believer. These two began a prayer meeting in one of the Sunday schools in the parish of Connor. Having his prayer answered in obtaining a spiritual partner, James McQuilkin asked the Lord to lead him to become acquainted with some more of His hidden ones. Soon after, the Lord gave him two more young men, who were believers previously, as far as he could judge. In autumn 1857, McQuilkin stated to these three young men, given to him in answer to believing prayer, what blessing he had derived from my *Narrative,* how it had led him to see the power of believing prayer. He proposed that they should meet for prayer to seek the Lord's blessing upon their various labors in the Sunday schools, prayer meetings, and preaching of the Gospel. Accordingly, in autumn 1857, these four young men met together for prayer in a small schoolhouse near the village of Kells, in the parish of Connor, every Friday evening. By this time, the great and mighty working of the Spirit in the United States, had become known, and McQuilkin said to himself, "Why may we not have such a blessed work here, seeing that God did such great things for Mr. Müller, simply in answer to prayer?"

On January 1, 1858, the Lord gave them the first remarkable answer to prayer in the conversion of a farm servant. He was taken into the number, and thus there were five who gave themselves to prayer. Shortly after, another young man, about twenty years old, was converted; there were now six. This greatly encouraged the other three who first had met with McQuilkin.

Others were then converted, who were also taken into the number; but only believers were admitted to these fellowship meetings, in which they read, prayed, and offered to each other a few thoughts from the Scriptures. These meetings and others for the preaching of the Gospel were held in the parish of Connor, County Antrim, Ireland. Up to this time, all was going on most quietly, though many souls were converted.

About Christmas 1858, a young man from Ahoghill who had come to live in Connor, and who had been converted through this little company of believers, went to see his friends at Ahoghill. He spoke to them about their own souls and the work of God in Connor. His friends desired to see some of these converts.

Accordingly, James McQuilkin, with two of the first who had met for prayer, went on February 2, 1859, and held a meeting at Ahoghill in one of the Presbyterian churches. Some believed, some mocked, and others thought there was a great deal of presumption in these young converts, yet many wished to have another meeting. This was held by the same three young men on February 16, 1859. Now the Spirit of God began to work, and to work mightily. Souls were converted, and from that time, conversions multiplied rapidly. Some of these converts went to other places and carried the spiritual fire, so to speak, with them. The blessed work of the Spirit of God spread in many places.

On April 5, 1859, McQuilkin went to Ballymena, held a meeting there in one of the Presbyterian churches, and on April 11 held another meeting in another of the Presbyterian churches. Several were convicted of their sins, and the work of the Spirit of God went forward in Ballymena.

On May 28, 1859, McQuilkin went to Belfast. During the first week, meetings were held in five different Presbyterian churches, and from that time, the blessed work began in Belfast. In all these visits, he was accompanied and helped by Jeremiah Meneely, one of the three young men who had first met with him, after he had read my *Narrative*. From this time, the work of the Holy Spirit spread further and further, for the young converts were used by the Lord to carry the truth from one place to another.

Such was the beginning of that mighty work of the Holy Spirit, which has led to the conversion of hundreds of thousands. Some of my readers will remember how in 1859 this fire was kindled in England, Wales, and Scotland; how it spread through Ireland, England, Wales, and Scotland; how the continent of Europe was more or less partaking of this mighty working of the Holy Spirit; how it led thousands to give themselves to the work of evangelists; and how up to the year 1874, not only the effects of this work, first begun in Ireland, are felt, but also more or less this blessed work is still going on in Europe generally. It is almost needless to add that in no degree is the honor due to the instruments, but to the Holy Spirit alone; yet these facts are stated in order that it may be seen what delight God has in answering abundantly the believing prayers of His children.

Müller's Marriage

In the third volume of the *Narrative,* Müller showed the ordering of God in his meeting with and subsequent marriage to his first wife, Miss Mary Groves.

In giving her to me, I acknowledge the hand of God; His hand was most noticeable, and my soul says, *"You are good, and do good"* (Ps. 119:68).

I refer to a few particulars for the instruction of others. When at the end of the year 1829, I left London to labor in the Gospel in Devonshire, a brother in the Lord gave a card to me that contained the address of a well-known Christian lady, Miss Paget, who resided in Exeter, in order that I should call on her since she was an excellent Christian. I took her address and put it into my pocket, but thought little of calling on her. For three weeks I carried this card in my pocket, without making an effort to see this lady, but at last I was led to do so. This was God's way of giving me my excellent wife.

Miss Paget asked me to preach the last Tuesday in the month of January 1830 in the room that she had prepared at Poltimore, a village near Exeter, and where Mr. A. N. Groves, afterward my brother-in-law, had preached once a month before he went out as a missionary to Baghdad. I readily accepted the invitation, since I longed to set forth everywhere the precious truth of the Lord's return, and other deeply important truths, with which, not long before, my own soul had been filled.

On leaving Miss Paget, she gave me the address of a Christian brother, Mr. Hake, who had a boarding school for young ladies and gentlemen at Northernhay House, the former residence of Mr. A. N. Groves, in order that I might stay there on my arrival in Exeter from Teignmouth. I went to this place at the appointed time. Miss Groves, who later became my beloved wife, was there. Mrs. Hake had been an invalid for a long time, and Miss Groves helped Mr. Hake in his great affliction by supervising his household matters.

My first visit led to my going again to preach at Poltimore, after the lapse of a month, and I stayed again at Mr. Hake's house. This second visit led to my preaching once a week in a chapel at Exeter. Thus I went, week after week, from Teignmouth to Exeter, each time staying in the house of Mr. Hake.

All this time my purpose had been not to marry at all, but to remain free for traveling about in the service of the Gospel. After some months, I saw that for many reasons, it was better for me, as a young pastor, under twenty-five years of age, to be married. The question now was, To whom will I be united? Miss Groves was before my mind, but the prayerful conflict was long before I came to a decision. I could not bear the thought that I would take away from Mr. Hake this valued helper, since Mrs. Hake continued to be unable to take on the responsibility of so large a household.

I prayed again and again. At last, this factor decided me: I had reason to believe that I had begotten an affection in the heart of Miss Groves for me, and that therefore I ought to make a proposal of marriage to her, however unkindly I might appear to act to my dear friend and brother Mr. Hake, and to ask God to give him a suitable helper to succeed Miss Groves. On August 15, 1830, I therefore wrote to her, proposing to her to become my wife, and on August 19, when I went over as usual to Exeter for preaching, she accepted my proposal.

The first thing that we did, after she accepted my proposal of marriage, was to fall on our knees and to ask the blessing of the Lord on our intended union. In about two or three weeks, the Lord, in answer to our prayer, found an individual who seemed suitable to act as housekeeper, while Mrs. Hake continued to be ill.

On October 7, 1830, we were united in marriage. Our marriage was of the most simple character. We walked to church, had no wedding breakfast, but in the afternoon had a meeting of Christian friends in Mr. Hake's house and commemorated the Lord's death. Then I drove off in the stagecoach with my beloved bride to Teignmouth, and the next day we went to work for the Lord. Simple as our beginning was, and unlike the habits of the world, for Christ's sake, so our godly aim has been to continue ever since. Now see the hand of God in giving me my dearest wife:

First, that address of Miss Paget's was given to me under the ordering of God. Second, I at last felt made to call on her, though I had long delayed it. Third, she might have provided a resting place with some other Christian friend, where I would not have seen Miss Groves. Fourth, my mind might have at last, after all, decided not to make a proposal to her, but God settled the matter by speaking to me through my conscience: "You know that you have begotten affection in the heart of this Christian sister by the way you have acted toward her, and therefore, painful though it may be to appear to act unkindly toward your friend and brother, you ought to make her a proposal." I obeyed. I wrote the letter in which I made the proposal, and nothing but one steady stream of blessing has been the result.

Advice on Choosing a Spouse

Let me add a word of Christian counsel. To enter into the marriage union is one of the most deeply important events of life. It cannot be too prayerfully treated. Our happiness, our usefulness, our living for God or for ourselves afterward, are often most intimately connected with our choice. Therefore, this choice should be made in the most prayerful manner. Neither beauty, nor age, nor money, nor mental powers, should be what prompts the decision, but first much waiting upon God for guidance should be used. Second, one should make it his wholehearted purpose to be willing to be guided by Him. Third, true godliness without a shadow of doubt should be the first and absolutely required qualification for a Christian with regard to a companion for life. In addition to this, however, it ought to be, at the same time, calmly and patiently weighed whether, in other respects, there is a suitableness.

For instance, for an educated man to choose an entirely uneducated woman is unwise, for however much on his part love might be willing to cover the defect, it will work very unhappily with regard to the children.

So I say to you, ask, and it will be given to you; seek, and you will find; knock, and it will be opened to you. For everyone who asks receives, and he who seeks finds, and to him who knocks it will be opened.
—Luke 11:9–10

Chapter Four

Conditions of Prevailing Prayer

Depend on Jesus

The first condition of prevailing prayer is an entire dependence upon the merits and mediation of the Lord Jesus Christ as the only ground of any claim for blessing. Consider the following verses:

And whatever you ask in My name, that I will do, that the Father may be glorified in the Son. If you ask anything in My name, I will do it.
(John 14:13–14)

You did not choose Me, but I chose you and appointed you that you should go and bear fruit, and that your fruit should remain, that whatever you ask the Father in My name He may give you. (John 15:16)

Forsake Sin

Second, there must be a separation from all known sin. God will not sanction sin. The Scripture says,

If I regard iniquity in my heart, the Lord will not hear. (Ps. 66:18)

Exercise Faith

Third, one must exercise faith in God's Word of promise as confirmed by His oath. Not to believe Him is to make Him out to be both a liar and a perjurer.

For when God made a promise to Abraham, because He could swear by no one greater, He swore by Himself, saying, "Surely blessing I will bless you, and multiplying I will multiply you." And so, after he had patiently endured, he obtained the promise. For men indeed swear by the greater, and an oath for confirmation is for them an end of all dispute. Thus God, determining to show more abundantly to the heirs of promise the immutability of His counsel, confirmed it by an oath, that by two immutable things, in which it is impossible for God to lie, we might have strong consolation, who have fled for refuge to lay hold of the hope set before us. This hope we have as an anchor of the soul, both sure and steadfast, and which enters the Presence behind the veil, where the forerunner has entered for us, even Jesus, having become High Priest forever according to the order of Melchizedek. (Heb. 6:13–20)

But without faith it is impossible to please Him, for he who comes to God must believe that He is, and that He is a rewarder of those who diligently seek Him. (Heb. 11:6)

He who says, "I know Him," and does not keep His commandments, is a liar, and the truth is not in him. (1 John 2:4)

Ask according to His Will

Fourth, ask in accordance with His will. Our motives must be godly. We must not seek any gift of God for selfish purposes.

Now this is the confidence that we have in Him, that if we ask anything according to His will, He hears us. (1 John 5:14)

You ask and do not receive, because you ask amiss, that you may spend it on your pleasures.
(James 4:3)

Persevere in Prayer

Fifth, there must be perseverance in prayer. There must be a waiting on God and a waiting for God, as the farmer has long patience to wait for the harvest.

Then He spoke a parable to them, that men always ought to pray and not lose heart, saying: "There was in a certain city a judge who did not fear God nor regard man. Now there was a widow in that city; and she came to him, saying, 'Get justice for me from my adversary.' And he would not for a while; but afterward he said within himself, 'Though I do not fear God nor regard man, yet because this widow troubles me I will avenge her, lest by her continual coming she weary me.'" Then the Lord said, "Hear what the unjust judge said. And shall God not avenge His own elect who cry out day and night to Him, though He bears long with them? I tell you that He will avenge them speedily. Nevertheless, when the Son of Man comes, will He really find faith on the earth?"

(Luke 18:1–8)

Therefore be patient, brethren, until the coming of the Lord. See how the farmer waits for the precious fruit of the earth, waiting patiently for it until it receives the early and latter rain.

(James 5:7)

Your word I have hidden in my heart, that I might not sin against You! Blessed are You, O LORD! Teach me Your statutes!
—Psalm 119:11–12

Chapter Five

Müller's Method
of Reading the Scriptures

The faithful reading of God's Word impacted George Müller's life in tremendous ways. Concerning the subject of Bible reading, Müller wrote,

I fell into the snare into which so many young believers fall—the reading of religious books in preference to the Scriptures. I could no longer read French and German novels, as I had formerly done, to feed my carnal mind, but still I did not replace those books with the best of all books. I read tracts, missionary papers, sermons, and biographies of godly persons. This last kind of book I found more profitable than others, and had they been well selected, or had I not read too much of such writings, or had any of them tended particularly to endear the Scriptures to me, they might have done me much good.

I never had been at any time in my life in the habit of reading the Holy Scriptures. When under fifteen years of age, I occasionally read a little of them at school; afterward God's precious Book was entirely laid aside, so that I never read one single chapter of it, as

far as I remember, until it pleased God to begin a work
of grace in my heart.

Reading the Word Increases Love for It

Now the scriptural way of reasoning would have
been: God Himself has condescended to become an
author, and I am ignorant about His precious Book,
which His Holy Spirit has caused to be written through
the instrumentality of His servants. It contains what I
ought to know, and the knowledge of which will lead
me to true happiness; therefore, I ought to read again
and again this most precious Book, this Book of books,
most earnestly, most prayerfully, and with much meditation. In this practice I ought to continue all the days
of my life.

I was aware, though I had read the Bible but little,
that I knew scarcely anything of it. But instead of acting thus, and being led by my ignorance of the Word of
God to study it more, my difficulty in understanding it
and the little enjoyment I had in it made me careless in
reading it (for much prayerful reading of the Word not
merely gives more knowledge, but also increases the
delight we have in reading it); and thus, like many believers, I practically preferred, for the first four years
of my new life in Christ, the works of uninspired men
to the oracles of the living God.

Reading the Word Fosters Spiritual Growth

The consequence was that I remained a babe, both
in knowledge and grace. I say in knowledge because all
true knowledge must be derived by the Spirit, from the

Word. And since I neglected the Word, I was for nearly four years so ignorant that I did not clearly know even the fundamental points of our holy faith.

This lack of knowledge most sadly kept me back from walking steadily in the ways of God. For it is the truth that makes us free (John 8:32), by delivering us from the slavery of *"all that is in the world; the lust of the flesh, the lust of the eyes, and the pride of life"* (1 John 2:16). The Word proves it; the experience of the saints proves it; and my own experience also most decidedly proves it. For when it pleased the Lord in August 1829 to bring me to the Scriptures, my life and walk became very different. And though even since that time I have very much fallen short of what I might and ought to be (see Romans 3:23), yet, by the grace of God, I have been enabled to live much nearer to Him than before.

If any believers read these words who prefer other books to the Holy Scriptures, and who enjoy the writings of men much more than the Word of God, may they be warned by my loss. I will consider this book to have been the means of doing much good, if it pleases the Lord through its instrumentality to lead some of His people no longer to neglect the Holy Scriptures, but to give them that preference that they have hitherto given to the writings of men.

My dislike of increasing the number of books available to readers would have been sufficient to deter me from writing these pages if I had not been convinced that this is the only way in which others may be benefited through my mistakes and errors. I was influenced by the hope that, in answer to my prayers, the reading of my experiences may be the means of leading them to value the Scriptures more highly and to make them the standard and guide of all their actions.

Reading the Word Teaches Spiritual Truths

If anyone should ask me how he may read the Scriptures most profitably, I would advise him that above all he should seek to have it settled in his own mind that God alone, by His Spirit, can teach him. Also, since he will be asking God for blessings, it is a beneficial idea to seek God's blessing before reading the Word, as well as during the reading of Scripture.

Moreover, he should have it settled in his mind that, although the Holy Spirit is the best and sufficient teacher, this Teacher does not always teach immediately when we desire it, and that, therefore, we may have to ask Him again and again for the explanation of certain passages. But He will surely teach us at last, if indeed we are seeking for light prayerfully, patiently, and with a view to the glory of God.

Read the Word Systematically

Also, it is of immense importance for the understanding of the Word of God, to read it systematically, so that every day we may read a portion of the Old and a portion of the New Testament, going on where we previously left off. The reasons to read the Bible in a systematic way are as follows:

This method is important, first, because it throws light upon the connection between the Old and New Testaments; a different method, where one habitually selects favorite chapters, will make it utterly impossible ever to understand much of the Scriptures.

Second, while we are in the body, we need a change, even in spiritual things; and this change the Lord has graciously provided in the great variety that is to be found in His Word.

Third, an orderly reading of the Word honors the glory of God. The leaving out of some chapters here and there is practically saying that certain portions are better than others, or that there are certain parts of revealed truth that are unprofitable or unnecessary.

Next, it may keep us, by the blessing of God, from erroneous views, since in reading regularly through the Scriptures, we are led to see the meaning of the whole. We are also kept from placing too much stress upon certain favorite views.

Fifth, the Scriptures contain the whole revealed will of God; therefore, we ought to seek to read from time to time through the whole of that revealed will. I fear that many believers in our day have not read even once through the whole of the Scriptures; yet in a few months, by reading only a few chapters every day, they might accomplish it.

Think about the Word

It is also of the greatest importance to meditate on what we read, so that perhaps a small portion, or, if we have time, the whole, may be meditated upon in the course of the day. Or a single portion of a book, or an epistle, or a gospel, through which we go regularly for meditation, may be considered every day, without causing one to be brought into bondage by this plan.

I have found scholarly commentaries to store the head with many notions and often also with the truth of God; but when the Spirit teaches, through the instrumentality of prayer and meditation, the heart is affected. The former kind of knowledge generally puffs up (1 Cor. 8:1), and is often renounced when another commentary gives a different opinion. It is often also found good for nothing, when it is to be carried out into practice. The latter kind of knowledge generally humbles, gives joy, leads us nearer to God, and is not easily reasoned away. Having been obtained from God, and thus having entered into our hearts, it becomes our own and is also generally carried out.

*For whoever does the will of God is My brother
and My sister and mother.*
—Mark 3:35

Chapter Six

How to Determine
the Will of God

Release Your Own Will

First, I seek at the beginning to get my heart into such a state that it has no will of its own in regard to a given matter. Nine-tenths of the trouble with people generally is at this point. Nine-tenths of the difficulties are overcome when our hearts are ready to do the Lord's will, whatever it may be. When one is truly in this state, it is usually just a little way before one discovers the knowledge of what God's will is.

Do Not Trust in Feelings

Second, having done this, I do not leave the result to feeling or simple impression. If so, I make myself liable to great delusions.

Look to the Spirit and the Word

Third, I seek the will of the Spirit of God through, or in connection with, the Word of God. The Spirit and the Word must be combined. If I look to the Spirit alone without the Word, I also lay myself open to great delusions. If the Holy Spirit guides us at all, He will do it according to the Scriptures and never contrary to them.

Consider the Circumstances

Next, I take into account providential circumstances. These often plainly indicate God's will in connection with His Word and Spirit.

Pray for God to Show You His Will

Fifth, I ask God in prayer to reveal His will to me so that I may understand it correctly.

Assess Your Peace regarding the Decision

Thus, through prayer to God, the study of the Word, and reflection, I come to a deliberate judgment according to the best of my ability and knowledge, and if my mind is thus at peace, and continues to be after two or three more petitions, I proceed accordingly. Both in trivial matters and in transactions involving most important issues, I have found this method always effective.

*Do not be conformed to this world,
but be transformed by the renewing
of your mind, that you may prove
what is that good and acceptable
and perfect will of God.*
—Romans 12:2

Chapter Seven

Proving the Acceptable Will of God

I t is very instructive and helpful to see the way in which Müller proved the acceptable will of the Lord when his heart was opened to pursue the enlargement of the orphan work, so that not only three hundred but one thousand orphans might be provided for.

December 11, 1850. The specific burden of my prayer is that God would be pleased to teach me His will. My mind has also been especially pondering how I could know His will satisfactorily concerning this specific request. I am sure that I will be taught. I therefore desire patiently for the Lord's time, when He will be pleased to shine on my path concerning this point.

God's Calm Assurance

December 26. Fifteen days have elapsed since I wrote the preceding paragraph. Every day since then, I have continued to pray about this matter, and that with a considerable measure of earnestness, by the help of God. Scarcely an hour has passed during these days, in which, while awake, this matter has not been more or less before me. But all without even a shadow of excitement. I converse with no one about it. To this point, I have not even done so with my dear wife. I still refrain from discussing it with others and deal with God alone about the matter, in order that no outward influence, and no outward excitement, may keep me from attaining a clear discovery of God's will.

I have the fullest and most peaceful assurance that He will clearly show me His will. This evening I have had again an especially solemn season of prayer to seek to know the will of God. But while I continue to entreat and beseech the Lord that He would not allow me to be deluded in this business, I may say I have scarcely any doubt remaining in my mind as to what will be the result, even that I should go forward in this matter.

As this, however, is one of the most momentous steps that I have ever taken, I judge that I cannot go about this matter with too much caution, prayer, and deliberation. I am in no hurry about it. I could wait for years, by God's grace, were this His will, before even taking one single step toward this thing, or even speaking to anyone about it; on the other hand, I would set to work tomorrow were the Lord to bid me to do so.

This calmness of mind, this having no will of my own in the matter, this only wishing to please my heavenly Father in it, this only seeking His and not my honor in it, this state of heart, I say, is the fullest assurance to me that my heart is not under a fleshly excitement, and that, if I am helped thus to go on, I will know the will of God fully. But, while I write thus, I cannot but add at the same time that I do crave the honor and the glorious privilege to be more and more used by the Lord. I served Satan much in my younger years, and I desire now with all my might to serve God during the remaining days of my earthly pilgrimage.

I am forty-five years and three months old. Every day decreases the number of days that I have to stay on earth. I therefore desire with all my might to work. Vast multitudes of orphans need to be provided for.

I desire that it may be yet more abundantly made clear that God is still the hearer and answerer of prayer, and that He is the living God now, as He ever was and ever will be, when He will, simply in answer to prayer, have condescended to provide me with a house for seven hundred orphans, and with means to support them. This last consideration is the most important point in my mind. The Lord's honor is the principal point with me in this whole matter; and just because that is the case, if He would be more glorified by my not going forward in this business, I would, by His grace, be perfectly content to give up all thoughts about another orphanage. Surely in such a state of mind, obtained by the Holy Spirit, You, O my heavenly Father, will not allow your child to be mistaken, much less to be deluded. By the help of God, I will continue further, day by day, to wait upon Him in prayer concerning this thing, until He directs me to act.

Trust in the Lord

January 2, 1851. I wrote the preceding paragraph a week ago. During this week, I have still been helped, day by day, and more than once every day, to seek the guidance of the Lord about another orphanage. The burden of my prayer has still been that He, in His great mercy, would keep me from making a mistake. During the last week, the book of Proverbs has come in the course of my Scripture reading, and my heart has been refreshed, in reference to this subject, by the following passages: *"Trust in the LORD with all your heart, and lean not on your own understanding; in all your ways acknowledge Him, and He shall direct your paths"* (Prov. 3:5–6).

By the grace of God, I do acknowledge the Lord in all my ways, and in this thing in particular. I have therefore the comfortable assurance that He will direct my paths concerning this part of my service, as to whether I will be occupied in it or not. Further, *"the integrity of the upright will guide them, but the perversity of the unfaithful will destroy them"* (Prov. 11:3). By the grace of God, I am upright in this business. My holiest purpose is to give glory to God. Therefore I expect to be guided aright.

The Scriptures also say, *"Commit your works to the LORD, and your thoughts will be established"* (Prov. 16:3). I do commit my works to the Lord; therefore, I expect that my thoughts will be established. My heart is more and more coming to a calm, quiet, and settled assurance that the Lord will condescend to use me yet further in the orphan work. "Here, Lord, is Your servant!" (See 1 Samuel 3:9–10; Isaiah 6:8.)

A Peaceful Decision

Müller wrote down eight reasons against and eight reasons for establishing another orphanage for seven hundred orphans. The following is his last reason for going ahead with the project:

I am peaceful and happy, spiritually, in the prospect of enlarging the work, as on former occasions when I was led to do so. This weighs particularly with me as a reason for going forward. After all the calm, quiet, prayerful consideration of the subject for about eight weeks, I am peaceful and happy, spiritually, in the purpose of enlarging the work. This, after all the heart-searching that I have had, and the daily prayer to be kept from delusion and mistake in this thing, and the faithful reading of the Word of God, would not be the case, I judge, if the Lord had not purposed to condescend to use me more than ever in His service.

I, therefore, on the grounds that the objections have been answered, and that these eight reasons for enlarging the work remain, come to the conclusion that it is the will of the blessed God that I, His poor and most unworthy servant, should yet more extensively serve Him in this work, which I am quite willing to do.

May 24. From the time that I began to write down the thoughts of my mind on December 5, 1850, until this day, ninety-two more applications for orphans needing homes have been received, and seventy-eight were already waiting for admission before. But this number increases rapidly as the work becomes more and more known.

On the basis of what has been recorded above, I purpose to go forward in this service, and to seek to build, to the praise and honor of the living God, another orphanage, large enough to accommodate seven hundred orphans.

Unless the LORD builds the house,
they labor in vain who build it.
—Psalm 127:1

Chapter Eight

God's Way

On October 9, 1875, Müller wrote about four essential aspects that contributed to his ability to rely on God.

This work has now been upheld for forty-two years. Though generally, year by year, it has been enlarged in one or more of its departments, God has never failed us, but has always supplied us with the needed provisions. How could our needs fail to be supplied if the work in which we are engaged is His work; if we are the persons to do this His work; if the time is come when we should be honored to do this His work; and if, at the same time, we trust in His power and willingness to help us?

God's Work

But these four different points need carefully to be examined. In the first place, we have to be sure that the work in which we are engaged is really the work of the Lord, and fully so. I stress this point because I have seen how, in order to keep persons from certain evil things, other evil things have been substituted. In the sight of some, these things may be less objectionable, yet they are of such a character that they are unworthy to be called God's work. How then could help from God be expected under such circumstances?

God's Person

Next we have to ascertain that we are the persons to be engaged in this work, which is really God's work, for we are not our own, but we are *"bought at a price"* (1 Cor. 6:19–20), the precious blood of the Lord Jesus.

Therefore, we may not spend our time, our talents, or our physical, mental, and spiritual strength as we please, but we have to seek to know whether the Lord would have us to be engaged in such a way or not.

God's Time

But even this is not enough. Still further, we have to seek to ascertain, by patient waiting upon God and watching His hand, whether His time has come that we should do this His work. How important these last two points are we have been clearly shown in Scripture regarding the building of the temple. The work was a good work, and quite according to the mind of Jehovah, but His time was not yet come that this work was to be done when David desired to build the temple; nor was David to be the man to do it, but his son, Solomon.

God's Resources

Suppose, last of all, not only that the work is God's work, but also that we are the persons to be engaged in this work. In addition, suppose that His own time has come when we are to be engaged in His work. Now, we have to trust in Him for all the help we need. If we do not do so, how can we expect for things to go well? And here I state that the necessary resources for which we who are involved in the orphan work in Bristol have to wait upon the Lord—great though they are, amounting to about forty-four thousand pounds yearly—are very far from all we need. We constantly have to look to the Lord for counsel and guidance in our difficulties; without His constant guidance, we would only make mistakes and take wrong steps.

My voice You shall hear in the morning, O Lᴏʀᴅ; in the morning I will direct it to You, and I will look up.
—Psalm 5:3

Chapter Nine

Advice on Rising Early

During my stay at Plymouth, I was incited again to rise early. I have not lost the results of this blessing since then. What led me to it was the example of the brother in whose house I was staying, and a remark that he made in speaking about the sacrifices mentioned in Leviticus. Just as one was not to offer a blemished animal as a burnt offering to the Lord (see Leviticus 22:19–20), so we should not give the worst part of our time to communion with the Lord.

I had been, on the whole, rather an early riser during former years. But since the nerves of my head had been so weak, I thought that, as the day was long enough for my strength, it would be best for me not to rise early, in order that the nerves of my head might have a longer period of quiet. Because of my weak physical condition, I rose only between six and seven, and sometimes after seven. For the same reason, I purposely acquired the habit of sleeping a quarter of an hour, or half an hour, after dinner, since I thought I found benefit from it in quieting the nerves of my head. In this way, however, my soul had suffered more or less every day, and sometimes considerably, as now and then unavoidable work came upon me before I had had sufficient time for prayer and the reading of the Word.

After I had heard the remark to which I have alluded, I determined that whatever my body might suffer, I would no longer let the most precious part of the day pass away while I was in bed.

By the grace of God, I was enabled to begin the very next day to rise earlier, and have continued to rise early since that time. I now allow myself about seven hours' sleep, which, though I am far from being strong, and have much to tire me mentally, I find is quite sufficient to refresh me. In addition to this, I gave up the practice of sleeping after dinner. The result has been that I have thus been able to procure long and precious seasons for prayer and meditation before breakfast. As to my body, and the state of my nervous system in particular, I have been much better since. Indeed, I believe that the very worst thing I could have done for my weak nerves was to have lain an hour or more longer in bed than I used to do before my illness, for it was the very way to keep me weak. Since this book may fall into the hands of some children of God who are not in the habit of rising early, I will make a few more remarks on the subject.

The Length of Rest

First, it might be asked, How much time should I allow myself for rest? The answer is that no rule of universal application can be given, since all persons do not require the same amount of sleep, and also the same persons, at different times, according to the strengths or weaknesses of their bodies, may require more or less. Yet, from what I can learn, it is the opinion of medical persons that men in health do not require more than between six and seven hours of sleep, and females no more than between seven and eight hours, so that it would be rather an exception for a man to require more than seven and a woman more than eight hours. But my decided advice, at the same time, is that children of God should be careful not to allow themselves too little sleep, as there are few men who can do with less than six hours of sleep and still be well in body and mind, and few females who can do with less than seven hours of sleep. For a long time, as a young man, before I went to the university, I went to bed regularly at ten and rose at four, studied hard, and was in good health; it is also true that since I have allowed myself only about seven hours, from the time of my visit to Plymouth in October 1839, I have been much better in body, and in my nerves in particular, than when I spent eight or eight and a half hours in bed.

The Reason for Rest

Second, if it is asked, Why should I rise early? the answer is, to remain too long in bed is a waste of time, which is unbecoming to a saint, who is bought by the precious blood of Jesus. All our time and all we have are to be used for the Lord. If we sleep more than is necessary for the refreshment of the body, we are wasting the time that the Lord has entrusted to us to be used for His glory, for our own benefit, and the benefit of the saints and the unbelievers around us.

I also believe that to remain too long in bed injures the body. Just as when we take in too much food, we are injured thereby, so it is in regard to sleep. Medical persons would readily agree that lying in bed longer than is necessary for the strengthening of the body does weaken it.

In addition, staying in bed too long injures the soul. It not merely keeps us from giving the most precious part of the day to prayer and meditation, but also leads to many other evils. All one needs to do is to experiment with spending one, two, or three hours in prayer and meditation before breakfast, either in his room or with the Bible in his hand in the fields, and one will soon discover the beneficial effects that early rising has upon the outward and inward man. I beseech all my brothers and sisters into whose hands this book may fall, and who are not in the habit of rising early, to make this test, and they will praise the Lord for having done so.

Do Not Delay

Finally, it may be asked, How will I set about rising early? My advice is to begin at once. Begin to rise early tomorrow. But do not depend upon your own strength. This may be the reason that, if before this you have tried to rise early, you have given it up. As surely as you depend upon your own strength in this matter, it will come to nothing. In every good work we depend upon the Lord, and in this thing we will feel especially how weak we are. If anyone rises early in order to give the time that he takes from sleep to prayer and meditation, let him be sure that Satan will try to put obstacles in the way.

Practical Advice

Trust in the Lord for help. You will honor Him if you expect help from Him in this matter. Give yourself to prayer for help, expect help, and you will have it.

However, in addition to this, practice the following means: Go to bed early. If you stay up late, you cannot rise early. Let no pressure of social engagements keep you from habitually going to bed early. If on occasion you are unable to go to bed early, you neither can nor should get up early since your body requires rest. Also, particularly keep in mind that for neither the body nor the soul is it the same thing to go to bed late and rise late, or to go to bed early and rise early. Even medical persons will tell you how injurious it is to spend the morning hours in bed; how much more important it is to retire early and to rise early in order to make sure of time for prayer and meditation before the business of the day begins. How important it is for your spiritual well-being to devote the part of your time when the mind and the body are most fresh to those spiritual exercises. In this way, one may obtain spiritual strength for the conflict, the trials, and the work of the day.

Let someone call you, if possible, at the time that you have determined before God that you will rise, or even better, buy an alarm clock, by which you may regulate almost to the minute the time when you wish to rise. Though I have very many times been awakened by the Lord, in answer to prayer, almost to the minute when I desired to rise, yet I thought it well to purchase an alarm clock to assist me in my purpose of rising early—not indeed as if it could give the least help without the Lord's blessing, for I could remain in bed notwithstanding the noise of the alarm clock, were He not to give me grace to rise. Look upon the clock simply as a means to help you. Rise immediately when you are awake. Do not remain a minute longer in bed; otherwise, you are likely to fall asleep again.

Do not be discouraged by feeling drowsy and tired as a result of your rising early. This feeling will soon wear off. After a few days, you will feel yourself stronger and fresher than when you used to lie in bed an hour or two longer than you needed. Always allow yourself the same hours for sleep. Make no change, unless sickness requires you to do so.

The effective, fervent prayer
of a righteous man avails much.
—James 5:16

Chapter Ten

Müller's Ninetieth Birthday

On the occasion of his ninetieth birthday, Müller, when speaking at Bethesda Chapel in Bristol, referred to his many travels and to his Christian experience. This account was given in the *Bristol Daily Press*:

He had traveled 200,000 miles by land and sea with his departed wife; had preached in 42 countries in Europe, America, Africa, Asia, and the six Australian colonies. Although formerly he used to suffer much from seasickness, he placed himself at God's disposal, and in all his journeys by sea had never suffered from sickness during these tours. He had crossed the Atlantic seven times, had been over the Red Sea five times, 16 times had been over the Mediterranean. He had crossed the Pacific Ocean and the Indian Ocean, and never once had he been in the least sick. See how good it was to be an obedient servant of Christ.

His mental powers were as clear as when he passed his examinations and wrote essays in Latin, French, and German, and had to pass examinations in Hebrew and Greek, mathematics, history, and the like. These examinations were 70 years and 6 months ago. How they should admire the Lord's kindness. Godliness was profitable even in that life.

He knew no way to begin, and no way to end, in speaking of the benefits the Lord had conferred on him. He had helped him in writing books, which God had blessed, and in the 42 countries, wherever he went, he met those who had known him a long time from his writings, and who were delighted to meet him face-to-face. See how God could use a miserable worm, who was only a wreck when brought to the knowledge of the Lord Jesus Christ, and who was that evening at the commencement of his 91st year.

For 69 years and 10 months he had been a happy man—a very happy man. That he attributed to two things. He had maintained a good conscience, not willfully going on in a course he knew to be contrary to the mind of God; he did not mean, of course, that he was perfect; he was poor, weak, and sinful. Second, he attributed it to his love for the Holy Scripture. Of late years, his practice had been to read through the entire Scriptures four times a year with application to his own heart, and with meditation, and at that day he was a greater lover of the Word of God than he was 66 years ago. The more the Bible was treated with carelessness and indifference, and the more it was reasoned away, the more he stuck close to it. It was this, and maintaining a good conscience, that had given him all those scores of years' peace and joy in the Holy Spirit.

His lord said to him, "Well done,
good and faithful servant;
you were faithful over a few things,
I will make you ruler over many things.
Enter into the joy of your lord."
—Matthew 25:21

Chapter Eleven

A God-Glorifying Testimony

I n the fifty-ninth report of the Scriptural Knowledge
Institution for Home and Abroad, James Wright, son-
in-law and successor to George Müller in the orphan
work, after giving the text of Müller's last will, wrote,

For the glory of God, whose grace made Mr. Müller
what he was, I record the fact that his personal estate
was sworn at £160 9s. 4d., consisting of books and
household furniture valued at £100 6s., and money in
his possession on the day of his death £60 3s. 4d. During his life he received by the gifts of God's children
and by bequests for his own absolute use, tens of thousands of pounds, but he counted it his joyful privilege
to regard the whole as committed to his stewardship.
Hence, he never laid up any monetary provision for the
future, either for himself personally, or for any mem-
ber of his family, but sought to *"lay up...treasures in
heaven"* (Matt. 6:20) by expending it in spreading in
various ways the knowledge of God's truth, or in minis-
tering to the necessities of the poor, *"especially to those
who are of the household of faith"* (Gal. 6:10).
By papers that have come into my hands, as his
executor, I find that, by acting habitually, through his
long Christian course, on the principle of systematic

giving as God was pleased to entrust him with means for his personal use, he was enabled to give away up to March 1, 1898, £81,490 18s. 8d., of which about £64,500 was put to the funds of the Scriptural Knowledge Institution, and about £17,000 to the poor, and to relatives when in need.

Accompanying the will, which was signed on March 16, 1895, was a private letter to myself dated fourteen months later, namely, May 13, 1896. In it he desired that I make known his concern that those who minister the Word of God may be led to bring before their hearers the deep importance of systematic giving for the work of God in proportion to the amount with which He is pleased to entrust His children.

A year before George Müller died, he was asked if he had always found the Lord to be faithful to His promises. This was Müller's reply:

Always. He has never failed me! For nearly seventy years, every need in connection with this work has been supplied. The orphans from the first until now have numbered ninety-five hundred, but they have never lacked a meal. Never! Hundreds of times we have begun the day without a penny in hand, but our heavenly Father has sent supplies by the moment they were actually required. There never was a time when we had no wholesome meal. During all these years, I have been enabled to trust in God, in the living God, and in Him alone. One million, four hundred thousand pounds have been sent to me in answer to prayer. We have needed as much as fifty thousand pounds in one year, and it has all come by the time it has really been needed.

No man on earth can say that I have ever asked him for a penny. We have no committees, no collections, no voting, and no endowments. All has come in answer to believing prayer. My trust has been in God alone; He has many ways of moving the hearts of men all over the world to help us. While I am praying He speaks to this one and another, on this continent and on that, to send us help.

...

Expect great things from God, and great things you will have. There is no limit to what He is able to do. Praise be forever to His glorious name! Praise Him for all! Praise Him for everything. I have praised Him many times when He has sent me sixpence, and I have praised Him when He has sent me twelve thousand pounds.

...

The great point is never to give up until the answer comes....The great fault of the children of God is that they do not continue in prayer; they do not go on praying; they do not persevere. If they desire anything for God's glory, they should pray until they get it. Oh, how good, kind, gracious, and generous is the One with whom we have to do!

...

I have met with many discouragements, but at all times my hope and confidence have been in God. On the word of Jehovah's promise has my soul rested. Oh, it is good to trust in Him; His Word never returns void (Isa. 55:11). He gives power to the faint, and to those who have no might He increases strength (Isa. 40:29).

*"I was hungry and you gave Me food;
I was thirsty and you gave Me drink;
I was a stranger and you took Me in;
I was naked and you clothed Me;
I was sick and you visited Me; I was in prison and
you came to Me." Then the righteous will answer
Him, saying, "Lord, when did we see You hungry
and feed You, or thirsty and give You drink?
When did we see You a stranger and take You in,
or naked and clothe You? Or when did we see You
sick, or in prison, and come to You?" And the King
will answer and say to them, "Assuredly, I say to you,
inasmuch as you did it to one of the least of these
My brethren, you did it to Me."*
—Matthew 25:35–40

Chapter Twelve

The Ministry Continues

Following George Müller's death in 1898, the work at the orphanages at Ashley Down continued in much the same way as it had in the past. James Wright, Müller's son-in-law, succeeded Müller as the Honorary Director. As Associate Director, Wright had been running the orphanages during Müller's years of missionary tours, so the work proceeded with the same principles established by George Müller. The tradition has followed that Associate Directors usually become Honorary Directors, which gives continuity to the administration of the work.

Honorary Directors

In 1905, George Frederic Bergin, one of the leaders at Bethesda Chapel, became the Honorary Director. He served until 1912, and then his son, William M. Bergin, assumed the responsibility until 1930. Subsequent Honorary Directors were Alfred E. Green (1930–1940); Thomas Tilsley (1940–1952); John McCready (1952–1958); and James J. Rose (1958–1986). Joseph Cowan served as Director from 1986–1988, and Robert L. Scott-Cook was Honorary Director from 1988 until

1994, when Julian P. Marsh took over the day-to-day running and oversight of the ministry. Currently, Mr. Scott-Cook is the Chairman of The George Müller Foundation. Writing in the 1998–99 Annual Report, Scott-Cook stated:

> The Foundation continues to hold George Müller's original vision to see God provide through prayer and faith. The daily prayer meetings together with the prayers of so many people around the world are at the heart of this work. God's faithful provision has been so evident again over another year. It has been wonderful to see faith and hope and love brought to so many broken hearts and broken lives, as the Foundation seeks to meet some of the current urgent spiritual, social, and physical needs in our society. Our vision is to bring together the three core values of faith, care, and evangelism.

The George Müller Foundation

The various ministries of the Müller work came to be called The George Müller Foundation in 1987. This title encompasses the three charities that reach out to serve people in distinctive ways: The Müller Homes for Children, The Müller Homes for the Elderly, and The Scriptural Knowledge Institution for Home and Abroad. The Foundation's statement of purpose is clearly biblical and God-honoring:

> The George Müller Foundation exists to glorify God by providing help for those with spiritual

146

and social needs. This is done in accordance with the Christian principle affirmed by George Müller that "the provision comes by prayer and faith without anyone being asked, whereby it might be seen that God is faithful still and hears prayer still."

Changing Times Bring New Direction

Although the founding principles have remained constant throughout the years, the specifics of the ministry have changed in order to meet the relevant needs of the times. In the early 1900s, the number of orphans gradually declined. Even though "part orphans," those who had lost only one parent, were admitted from about the turn of the twentieth century, and in the 1940s the decision to accept illegitimate children was made, the overall number of orphans dwindled to the point where first one house and then a second were closed. During the Second World War, two buildings were used to house GI's.

Several societal changes brought about the decline in the number of orphans and contributed to the eventual close of the Ashley Down structures: the improvement in public health, a decline in the death rate, better legislation exercised over workplace conditions, a reduction in family size, a rise in the need for facilities to care for children who had been neglected or abused rather than orphaned, more governmental involvement in providing care for children in need, changing attitudes toward ways of caring for children, and increased expenses for maintaining and updating the large buildings to house the orphans.

By the 1940s, a national reappraisal of child care led the Trustees of the Müller homes to seek God's direction for the future of the orphanages. They were led to close the homes and eventually sell them in 1958 to the local education authority. Commenting on the concern of the Foundation to maintain its relevancy, Julian Marsh, Chief Executive of The George Müller Foundation, wrote,

> It has always been the desire of the leadership of the work to know clearly from God if the "season" for the work had come to an end. This question was asked during this period, "Lord, is this the end of the work?" Each time it has been seen to be God's will for the work to continue, albeit in a new form but still seeking to fulfill the key principles of the work.

During George Müller's lifetime, the orphanages provided a Christian answer for the care of orphans who would have faced the bitter alternatives of death or the workhouse. The children received an education that some criticized as being "above their station." But George Müller did not agree. He even employed a school inspector to ensure that the standards of education for the orphans were kept high. The average percentage of all the children in 1885 on their yearly examination, which covered six subjects, was 91.1 percent. Because Müller cared for and educated the boys until they were fourteen and the girls until they were seventeen before seeking employment for them, he was accused by some of robbing factories, mills, and mines of their potential workforce. However, because of improved state schools* and better social conditions in general, the kind of care needed for children today is different from what it was during Müller's lifetime. During the last half of the nineteenth century, the Müller homes were ahead of their times in many ways, but by the 1930s, they were becoming to some extent an anachronism.

When the five large homes at Ashley Down were sold, smaller properties that housed ten to twelve children in a family setting were purchased. Married couples, with the help of two assistants and part-time domestic workers, became houseparents to the children. These smaller family group homes were located in Bristol, as well as in Clevedon and Weston-super-Mare. Another home operated in Backwell, and a vacation home was purchased in Minehead. No longer was the emphasis on formal education, because the children all attended local state schools. Since many of the children came from broken homes and had been emotionally deprived in some way, the focus of the ministry was to provide an atmosphere where the children could become healthy, both physically and emotionally. Additionally, the children's spiritual needs have always been and continue to be of primary concern.

Day Care and Family Support Centers

By the late 1970s, the Trustees felt that even the family group homes were not meeting the ever changing

---

* In the United Kingdom, state schools are the equivalent of American public schools. Public schools in the UK refer to independent schools where students pay fees to attend (like Eton).

needs brought about by societal changes. Because local agencies were placing children in foster care with individual families, the needs of children were once again shifting. Seeking the continued guidance of God, the Trustees established a Day Care Center in Weston-super-Mare. Three criteria are used in assessing a child's eligibility for this program. Any one of the following factors would qualify a child for this care: if an environmental problem caused by inadequate housing or limited resources for recreation put the child's health at risk; if a preschool-aged child needed care because of the ill health or emotional instability of a parent; or if a single parent was forced to work in order to provide for his or her child.

In addition to the Day Care Center, several Family Support Centers were opened in the Bristol area. These centers help counter the attack on the family today, providing varied kinds of assistance to over two hundred families each week. In addition, two school workers were appointed in 1987 to promote the Good News of Jesus Christ in the schools in and around Bristol.

The Work in Schools

The work among school-aged children and youth has continued to expand. After conducting self-esteem seminars, Müller educational staff identified students at risk of being alienated from classmates and more likely to drop out of school without adequate training for their futures. Small group programs have been initiated to address the needs of these students, and positive changes have been noted by the staff, the students, and their teachers. The Foundation's holistic approach to reaching out to school students includes the following aspects of ministry:

- seminars to address the issue of bullying
- mentoring
- safe haven rooms available at break times
- residential camps
- church-related youth events
- religious education lessons covering topics such as Christian Belief, Commitment, Drugs, Relationships, Sanctity of Life, Easter, Death, Baptism
- classroom support
- training for local church workers

A Committed Purpose

Although the children's work has changed in appearance today, its purpose is essentially the same: to glorify God and to look to Him to provide the health and healing needed by people. One of the ways in which The George Müller Foundation has multiplied its resources is by teaming up with local churches and providing support, encouragement, training, and resources. The following list of the typical activities offered by professional teams of staff demonstrates the wide range of help needed and given:

- provide day care
- supervise church-based parent and toddler groups
- conduct self-esteem groups for schoolchildren
- give support to parents' groups

- teach Bible study for parents
- lead children's bereavement groups
- organize play groups
- coordinate anger management groups for parents
- monitor self-help groups for parents
- offer counseling
- provide advocacy help for parents
- assist in homes, including cooking, family management, and general skills
- speak at school assemblies or clubs, or serve as a teacher's assistant in community-based elementary schools
- run after-school clubs
- assess community needs
- meet with representatives of the statutory agencies

And the list goes on.

Associated Ministries

In addition to the varied work carried out by the staff and volunteers of The George Müller Foundation, other associated ministries work in partnership with them. The Foundation actively supports and encourages the work of the following ministries:

- the Caleb Project, a Christian drug rehabilitation program
- Care Housing, a Christian discipling organization that provides supported housing for young people

- Crisis Centre Ministries, a Christian agency that works with street people and addicts, offering hope, shelter, training, and discipling
- Network Counseling and Training, a Christian agency that provides counseling to those in need, as well as training for counselors

The Müller Homes for the Elderly

Besides the multiple ministries geared toward children and their parents, the needs of the elderly have not been overlooked. Tilsley House in Weston-super-Mare was founded in 1983 and provides residential home care for twenty-four persons. Although the rooms are well furnished, residents are encouraged to bring some of their own belongings to make their rooms more personalized. The house has its own garden, and Clarence Park is directly opposite the property. Churches, stores, and the beach are all within walking distance. A garden to tend and planned activities are also available for residents. The 1998–99 Annual Report for The George Müller Foundation states that "in 1986 the average age of permanent residents at Tilsley House was 77.71 years, whereas twelve years later in 1998, the average age of residents was 86.52 years." With increased longevity, the need for Christian care for the elderly will continue to grow.

When the neighboring property to Tilsley House became available, the Trustees purchased it and converted it into eight apartments (flats) overseen by a "warden," or guardian. Tranquil House, as it is called, provides an additional opportunity to meet the needs of the elderly. The Trustees are seeking the Lord's continued guidance as they strive to expand the ministry to the aged in the Bristol area.

The Scriptural Knowledge Institution

Another aspect of the ongoing influence of George Müller is the distribution of Christian literature. With the founding on March 5, 1834, of the Scriptural Knowledge Society (later to become SKI, the Scriptural Knowledge Institution for Home and Abroad), George Müller established four main objectives. (The fifth objective, added later, was to become a primary focus as he sought to meet the ever increasing needs of orphaned children.) The third purpose of the SKI was to circulate the Holy Scriptures. Because of his commitment to spread the Good News of God's Word to the world, Müller started a Bible warehouse and bookshop in Bristol. In 1852, the Bible and Tract Warehouse and Bookshop changed locations to Park Street in Bristol. This ministry continued until the shop was destroyed by fire during the Second World War. A new store, the Evangelical Christian Literature, was opened on Park Street in 1957. Two other branches opened—one in 1974 in Bath, and one in 1984 in Weston-super-Mare.

In the early 1990s, a decision was made to sell the shops to other Christian booksellers. The shops in Bath were first sold to Scripture Union, and the stores in Bristol and Weston-super-Mare were taken over by Send the Light, an extension ministry of Operation Mobilization. All of the operation of the bookstores, including the ones in Bath, has since become a part of Send the Light, and they trade under the name Wesley Owen Books and Music.

These stores not only sought to fulfill the third objective of the SKI, but also contributed to the fourth objective as well: to help supply the needs of missionaries and missionary schools. A portion of the profits from the bookstores was sent to missionaries in order to provide Bibles for those who did not have them. In addition to these monies, support of missionaries is ongoing. In 1998, over £500,000 was sent to support missionaries both in the United Kingdom and throughout the world.

Care for Missionaries Continues

The objective of supplying the needs of missionaries and missionary schools is still very much a part of The George Müller Foundation. One only has to glance through the most recent Annual Report to see the faces and names of missionaries around the world who are being supported in prayer and with financial help. The missionary heart and zeal of George Müller continue to direct the ministry decisions and focus of the Foundation today. God's name is still being *"exalted among the nations"* (Ps. 46:10), in part because of the support being given by the Foundation to missionaries intent on spreading the Gospel message throughout the earth.

The Future of the Ministry

In evaluating its role in the twenty-first century, the staff of the Müller Foundation has prayerfully sought God's guidance. In order to maintain its threefold purpose of care, faith, and evangelism, they will seek to shift gradually from directly providing services to joining in partnership with local churches and other associated ministries to maximize their efforts to meet people's needs. More training will be offered to church members to enable them to reach out into their communities. The Director's Report through February 1999 emphasizes the focus on equipping others for ministry:

> It has become increasingly evident that churches have much potential in expressing the love and care of God to children and families. Our efforts will increasingly be focused on helping and training them to do so and to share in partnership together to see a wider group of people experiencing quality care. ...Our commitment to quality care for children and families will continue as we forge more and more relationships with churches, and we are confident that the number and range of people whom we may be able to serve will continue to grow considerably.

The hallmark of The George Müller Foundation has been its faithfulness to maintain the simple but profound practice begun by George Müller over a century and a half ago: to glorify God, to look to Him for His provision, and to serve others with the love that He has so generously bestowed on us.

One of the outstanding testimonies to the faithfulness of God and the godly example of George Müller comes from a former resident of the Müller homes. She said,

> The greatest thing that has ever happened to me was at the Müller Homes because there I

learned about the Lord Jesus. Through the teaching that had been put into my heart as a child, I gave that same heart to the Lord one day, and I have never regretted it.

Likewise, George Müller never regretted his decision to follow Christ and to trust in His promises. His legacy remains and continues to touch lives because of the committed Christians who follow the godly example of a man who took God at His Word.

For Further Information...

I f you are interested in learning more about George
Müller and the work of The George Müller Founda-
tion, you are invited to contact the Chief Executive,
Julian P. Marsh, at:

Müller House
7 Cotham Park
Bristol BS6 6DA
England

Telephone: 0117 924 5001
Fax: 0117 924 4855
Web site: http://www.mullers.org
E-mail: admin@mullers.org

You are also encouraged to visit the museum at
Müller House, which is open Monday through Friday
from 10:00 A.M. until 4 P.M. (except for Bank Holidays).
Whenever possible, it is requested that you give ad-
vance notice of your visit to the Chief Executive. Additional books by and about George Müller, leaflets,
picture postcards, bookmarks, and a video are available
from the Foundation.